T0198872

SILENT WORLD OF VISIONS

"THE CHOSEN DAUGHTER OF ZION"

MOSEBODI BETTY METSWAMERE

authorHOUSE®

AuthorHouse™
1663 Liberty Drive
Bloomington, IN 47403
www.authorhouse.com
Phone: 1-800-839-8640

Published by AuthorHouse   03/30/2012

ISBN: 978-1-4685-7488-3 (sc)
ISBN: 978-1-4685-7487-6 (hc)
ISBN: 978-1-4685-7486-9 (e)

Library of Congress Control Number: 2012905952

TABLE OF CONTENTS

INTRODUCTION

This is a true story of a young girl who grew up being typically unsociable and different in a rural area called Bodibe in Lichtenburg within the North West Province of South Africa. Her whole life was characterized by emotional and spiritual loneliness which denied her of enjoying her childhood. She spent most of her life communicating with God her "imaginary friend". She had a friend that most children never had. Her personal relationship with God grew more and more from childhood until she came to realize that her life was not the same as that of children of her age. She spent her whole life in a totally different spiritual world which captured her concentration. Emotional conflict and pain over clouded her life when she started to realize that she had spiritual gifts that she had never wanted as a child. God called her to join the Zion Christian Church to prepare her to serve his purpose. After preparing her, God led her to join the African Apostolic religious groups by uniting them as one happy family, and establish St. Mary's Inter Denominational Ministry to spread the message of hope, faith, and salvation.

Special dedications

1. To my imaginary friend "God" of Mount Zion, whose presence in my whole life gave me a wonderful story to share with the nations.
2. To Bairley Roberts, a writing Coach at Saint Michael's College and to my late friend, Michael Mosimanegape Senosi for his immense and valuable support in the community empowerment projects.
3. To my editor, Ndianko Ndao, MATESOL student at Saint Michael's College, for his endurance, understanding, and kindheartedness in making this piece of writing a great success.
4. To Choabi Koba Alina and Mailwane Monyela for their support and encouragement.
5. To the large happy family of St. Mary's Inter Denomination Ministry for giving me their endless support at all times in serving the purpose of the Almighty, and for whispering my name in their prayers.
6. To my devoted parents, Grace and Matthews Maotoane
7. To my beloved brother and sister, George and Florence Maotoane.
8. To my precious children, Tshedimosetso and Keamogetse, for being considerate and accepting other children who are under my care, and those who lived in our home.
9. To the Youth and all the children of Agisanang Hiring Services, Agisanang children's home and Regololosegile drop in Centre.

10. All the parents, educators and learners of Legae-thuto Primary School.

11. To the following youth and children who gave me the honor of being their sister, mother and guardian: Manaledi(late), Hidy, Maserame, Ester, Junior, Fikile, Segametsi, Tidimalo, Lebogang, Mosenene, Bonolo, Papi, Konosi, Tumi, Remo, Abel, Mashadi, Lerato, Kegomoditswe, Thabiso, Thuso, Tshidiso(late), Lesego, Thabang, Christian, Lucrecia, Peter, and all others.

CHAPTER 1

GOD: SIBU'S IMAGINARY FRIEND

"Once we focus our attention into the spiritual world, we feel that there is no joy in this physical world", said the little girl sobbing. Our place of joy is where our father lives". The most beautiful toys and clothes had no meaning and value in her life. Sibu's total focus was stolen by the world of the unseen. Her desire to live in a world of harmony turned her into a total alien in this real world. She was so lonely and sad that it seemed she had no friends at all. Her mind was totally consumed by the spiritual world; a world she deeply believed was her home. Nobody knew how it happened that Sibu became part of this strange world, which is feared by the wise and the bravest men. Only a few elders could notice that this little girl was different from other children. "Do not be afraid for, I am with you", these words echoed in her ears all the time. Quietness and confidence was her strength. Beautiful clothes, shoes and toys never worried her much. She knew she didn't belong to this world; her home was in the spiritual world where her imaginary friend lived.

Sibu would seldom spend much time with other children during her childhood, even though they liked her so much. Playing with other children had never been her priority. She preferred to be alone and communicate with her imaginary friend most of the time. The joy she had or felt when she was with her imaginary friend was beyond measure. She involved him in every little thing she did. It even seemed as if her spiritual friend was her only pillar of hope and strength. This was unusual for a child of her age. In her heart she always believed that if the whole world had been filled with people like her friend; it would have been a much happier place to live in. Her isolation from other children and this physical world presented to her the effects of quietness and assurance forever. She knew that she had to be still and acknowledge the presence of the Almighty.

Her spiritual and personal connection to her friend was one of her secrets. She had an inner teacher, the greatest spirit guard and a caring friend. Within her friend she found silence and peace that none of the children of her age could enjoy. This was indeed a privilege. At times when she was among people she lost concentration. Those who understood her would notice her when she would start saying "m . . . m . . . yes . . . . Ok I see!" Then, they would know that her mind was miles and miles way. The further her mind was, the more harmony, peace and silence she felt. Her dearest friend isolated her more and more from other children. Delicious food, chocolates, sweets, and ice cream meant something different to her. She didn't eat much, especially things that were too salty, or too sweet. She cared a lot for her hair mostly. She liked to look pretty and smart at all times. Maybe it's because cleanliness is next to Godliness.

Sibu and her grandmother, Oudora got closer and closer every day. They had one common goal, which was to live a life that would please their heavenly Father. Every day they prayed, sang, and read the bible together. Oudora was the name that was commonly used by the villagers to call Sibu's granny. She was very old and couldn't read books or even write; Sibu read the bible and folktales to her granny. At times they sang together. Oudora was very old, and she was unable to go to their church of the Roman Catholic. Sibu was the only link that kept her granny spiritually connected and active. She attended the church regularly and brought Oudora all important church announcements.

Every Sunday when she returned from church she would read the bible scriptures of the day and shared them with her Granny. When Oudora visited the church Sibu would carry her chair on her head and walk on her granny's side. When her grandmother was tired she would sit on that chair for some minutes. After feeling better they would continue with the journey to the church. After all those occasional breaks they finally arrived at the church, and after church they would return home the same way. This was not a problem to Sibu, she couldn't even feel tired of carrying her granny's special chair. She loved her granny more than anything else.

Sibu was a very brave and courageous little girl who always had high hopes and dreams about her future. Oudora's family had nothing shiny of this material world but community members envied them. Oudora regarded Sibu as her shiny bright lamp that shone through with the brightness that community members couldn't ignore. She always shared her light with other children, and especially her grandmother. Her beautiful voice made her more special. She sang in the local church choir of St Patrick Apostolic Church. Her granny knew that she had to let her attend choir practice during certain days of the week. Singing and praying made her feel connected to the spiritual world. Her little secret world of impossibilities was one kind of a world whose experiences she would never share with anyone including her own granny; it was her deepest secret.

One day Sibu had a special talk with her friend, and she said: "Father, if you really love me you would never take my granny away from me, you would let her live longer than other grannies". Her friend, never replied, he remained silent. She took a round enamel dish filled it with corn grains and she said: "Father if you really love me, please let my granny live many years equal to the number of grains in this bowl", unfortunately her friend still remained silent. Sibu got sad for the whole day, for she knew what the silence meant. She knew that one day her granny would be called to live in the bosom of Jesus Christ. She tried to convince her friend in advance not to take her granny away from her. She told him that if He took her granny away, she would have no one to live with. She was so glued to her granny that she did not want to imagine life without her. Oudora always regarded Sibu as her light bright light lighting her life.

The St. Patrick Apostolic church once sent an elder relative to request from Oudora to move Sibu from the Roman Catholic Church, but Oudora refused. Oudora told him that Sibu was her only link to the Roman Catholic Church. The man tried his best to convince her stating that his church's elders noticed that the little girl had spiritual gifts and a good healing voice. They needed her as part of the church so as to groom her. They felt Sibu was one of the chosen children whom they regarded as the most powerful instrument of the Lord. An instrument that the Lord could use to bring hope and change lives. Nothing that the man said could make Oudora change her mind.

They regarded Sibu as a means to connect to God, and wished to mentor her spiritually. Sibu's spirituals gifts were noticed when she volunteered in the St. Patrick Apostolic church choir concerts. She would go back home with her pockets full of coins after those concerts, for her voice was so unique that no one could resist. She sang so beautifully that audience stood up from their seats: walked to the front and gave her money to appreciate her golden voice, especially at her age. The innocent sweet healing voice of this nine year old little girl moved the hearts of many concert attendees, so much that some couldn't even hold their tears. This singing talent of Sibu made villagers and other children to adore her more. Every child wanted to be part of Sibu's life, and instead she wanted to be part of her spiritual world. What Sibu herself didn't know and wouldn't want to hear about by that time was that she had spiritual gifts. She didn't understand that having a strong relationship with God as her" imaginary friend", and at her age was quite unusual. She believed she was as ordinary as other children.

Oudora loved God with all her heart. She dedicated her whole life serving Him, helping and loving everyone; she was also a role model to Sibu. Every night Sibu gathered with all other children in Oudora's bedroom for a prayer. Nobody could easily go to bed in Oudora's house without praying. In her home she welcomed everyone: the poor, the disabled and the children. No one could go hungry or thirsty unless there was no food or tea. One could say that she had a gift of encouraging and showing kindness to others. She gave generously to everyone and loved them genuinely. Oudora did everything in the name of the Almighty. She knew in her heart that nothing she did for the Lord was ever useless.

Sibu loved and trusted God to the extent that she had her own secret silent prayers which were very long. Her prayers were more like a long silent conversation with her Imaginary friend. When Oudora and other children thought she was asleep: she wasn't. Every night she had a special prayer and relied heavily on it. She knew that this prayer was different from the one she said with other children. When she prayed, tears streamed down her cheeks as if she was troubled. These tears were an indication of peace and warmth that she felt when talking to her own Father. She loved her silent prayers for she knew that accepting silence is the first step towards intimacy with God.

Sibu valued the church, prayer, and silence as her only connection to the unseen world. Praying linked her soul, mind, and heart to God. Praying was one thing she could not resist or live without. It strengthened her friendship with her imaginary friend. It was an amazing experience for her to share her childhood worries and joyful moments with her kindhearted friend. Her spiritual friend never judged her in any way. He was always there to listen. Sibu was introduced to this friend of hers by her own granny. Oudora always regarded the Lord as her personal friend too.

She would say and repeat the following prayers seven times every night before going to bed: our Father who art in heaven, the Lord is my shepherd, the apostolic creed, and Hail Mary for twelve times. The reason she said these prayers several times, was that she had a covenant with her Friend to save all these prayers. She requested Him to consider all her prayers for future reference especially on days that she would be too old or too busy to pray. She asked him to spread each prayer to cover for nights and days when she has grown up and is not able to pray. She was very clever and always planned ahead. She loved God with all her heart, and didn't even think of upsetting him in any possible way. She prayed for her future so to remain safe under God's protection. Sibu was aware that her family background was poor and her mother's income was too low, that she might not afford studying at the University. She then dedicated part of her prayers to her future career. She prayed God to make it possible that when she completes her High school; she be admitted at a nursing college as it was free at that time.

In fact she was not in favor of nursing; she needed it as a stepping stone to a social work degree at the University. She knew that she would be trained as a nurse, receive a monthly stipend and save for her University studies. Social work was her dream career. She had the passion to help the poor and change lives just like her granny. Professions like teaching, spiritual healing, and being a priest had never been part of her dreams. All she thought of as a child was that God loved her so much that He would let her decide on how she should live her own life. Oudora never taught her that God's ways and plans are totally different from our own, that He knows better what is good for each of us. We have the right to ask, but we do not have the authority to tell him what to do.

Sibu was from a poor family; her mother couldn't take care of her appropriately. She left her when she was two months old with her grandmother, so she could return to work in Johannesburg as a domestic servant. It was not easy for Grace to leave her baby behind; however, she knew her baby was in good hands and would be fine with Oudora who also brought her up. During those times, there were no maternity leaves for domestic servants. Grace was forced to return to work in Johannesburg so as to keep the family surviving.

She didn't earn much, but the little amount of money she would earn was enough to keep the whole family living. Oudora's family was one of those who had nothing but the love of Jesus Christ. The love of Christ shone through their hearts all the time. One could regard Oudora as a village candle that shone with the brightness that attracted many villagers to her. She was more like a candle that shared its light with many. When people felt helpless, hopeless, and hungry they knew

Oudora's place had everything they needed. None of the villagers would leave her house sad or starving.

The family was so poor that Sibu went to school with holes in her shoes. Other learners and educators could not even notice that. She patched her shoes to avoid being prickled by small stones, thorns, and other sharp objects. Oudora could only afford buying low cost shiny plastic shoes that lasted for not more than six months. Shoe polishing was not a concern to Sibu. She would apply Vaseline that would make them shine all the time. These kinds of shoes were called plastic or Vaseline shoes. Children from wealthy families would never wear them because it was considered shameful. Since Sibu's focus was not on this material world, she never cared. Her whole attention was captured by the world of the unseen. She never had a sense of belonging to this material world. There were days when she would go to school without any lunch box, not because there was nothing to eat, but because the type of meals the family used to eat wasn't good enough to be taken to school and could cause mockery from other children.

Oudora's yard was a place where many children could gather and play peacefully. Sibu was treated like a queen by other children because she had many beautiful toys that they didn't have. They would help her to carry her big bag of toys as well as her special small chair when they decided to play. Every child wanted to be her friend, and none of the children teased her as they knew Oudora would pinch them. However, Sibu was so kind and generous and there was no reason for other children to tease her. Her mother used to work for the wealthy generous white families who often offered her beautiful toys to give to Sibu. All those beautiful toys explained why she was always accompanied and followed by other children, and she knew how to share and play with all of them.

It was clear that one day she would become a good leader, but she never spent much time playing. She enjoyed being alone in order to chat with her imaginary friend. She had an unusual habit: One would think she was having a rest during the day, only to find her mind was busy communicating with her imaginary friend. In most instances her imaginary friend revealed many secrets about her future through dreams. This was one of her most amazing experiences ever. She used to have dreams that connected her to the spiritual world; dreams in which she would find peace with herself, but she kept all of them to herself.

Oudora used to prepare a special African traditional beer that she sold to the villagers, but her generosity made it impossible to make profit. She took long hours brewing and at the end of the day she was left with nothing; she worked at a loss. Lots of people came on days the traditional beer was sold; everyone knew before they bought the beer that they would get a free liter to taste. It was her style of welcoming customers. If she prepared twenty liters of beer, then ten would be sold and ten liters would be for free. Oudora was too old to pour beer for customers. She delegated some people to help with pouring the beer for those who wanted to buy, and unfortunately they used to cheat.

The one whom she sent to pour the beer would take a sip first or even more as she couldn't be seen by anyone. The beer was kept in a separate room. My grandmother noticed that and introduced a new way of stopping them from drinking her beer when pouring for customers. Whenever she sent someone she asked them to sing, for she knew that they could not sing and drink at the same time. Whenever she asked someone to help with pouring the beer, and that the person stopped singing, she knew that they were drinking. This new method worked very well.

Each and every day of my life with granny was filled with joy and happiness. She treated me more like the only baby she ever had. In fact, I was not the only child in the family. There were other children living with us, but I stole all her love. She considered me as the queen of birds. At times, she would tell me the story of the smallest bird that was the cleverest of them all. Perhaps I got cleverer and cleverer because she believed in me. Whenever she became sick, I would give her water and touched her, and she would feel better. She even wanted me to become a nurse after I had completed my schooling. She believed that I was good at looking after her. She was strongly convinced that I had some power that made her feel better whenever she had been sick. I never told her that I didn't like nursing or anything that had to do with physical or spiritual healing.

One night, I had a vision: my Heavenly Father revealed my future. In that vision I saw a very long step ladder standing up from the ground up to the sky. I saw myself climbing up with my primary school learners. Unfortunately, one of them was not able to climb with us; he remained on the ground. As I went up and up, I found myself among my middle school classmates, and later on, I was with High school learners. We arrived at a place which was more like a kitchen. This area was very high up in the sky. When I looked down I couldn't see a thing because it was extremely dark and scary. It was even frightening to look down to earth. When we arrived in the kitchen, I was hoping to relax and have food, for I was very tired, and my legs were aching. When I was about to sit down and rest a bit, I could hear the echo of my imaginary friend's voice telling me: "My child you haven't reached your destination of your career path yet, you still need to move farther up, and I will be with you". I continued with my journey going up, and I was too exhausted. I can't remember how far exactly I walked up.

"Sibu! Sibu, Sibu! It's time to go to school" my grandmother called. I woke up and jumped out of my bed. The stepladder indicated my career path. One learner who couldn't climb up died after two years. He was only at the primary level. He never progressed to the middle school.

It is indeed true that God's plans are totally different from our own. What is impossible with us is possible with him. I always thought that it would be impossible for me to study at the University immediately after completing my High Schooling because of my poor family background. I applied at many nursing colleges, hoping for admission but I had always been rejected. I believed in God as my imaginary friend and trusted him, but I never bothered myself asking him to help me to gain direct entry at the University, as I thought it was impossible.

In those days no one could tell me that God had a special plan about my life. If Only I had known that having him as my imaginary friend was a blessing, and it would have been more than enough. I didn't know that He had already planned great things about my life; and had created me for a purpose. All I needed by that time was to be strong and courageous. There was no need to panic about my future. I was blind to remember that, even the Lord's Prayer "Our Father" that I used to say seven times every night says: "Give us our daily bread", not give us bread for tomorrow.

I used to worry a lot about my future. The presence of the Lord by my sides was not enough for me to be patient and wait for Him to act. The bible says "Wise farmers wait patiently for the rain in the fall and in the spring: they eagerly look for the valuable harvest to ripen". All my granny could tell me was that "Sibu, you are a blessing to my life; you are the cleverest child ever, and you are my candle", and that made me feel so good and more motivated. My love for my grandmother grew more and more that I even wished we lived together forever. Unfortunately I had to leave her behind, and travel to Johannesburg to my mother, so I could be closer to educational institutions. Leaving my Granny behind was the most difficult thing I ever had to do. What I didn't know was that the goodbye we said to each other was the last one. The painful goodbye I might not easily forget. "Bye granny" I waved, "Bye Sibu, please take care of yourself in the city and know that I will always love you and pray for you" she waved back. We both couldn't hold our tears, and it was like we knew that it was our last goodbye. I now believe that some goodbyes are easier and some are harder. I promised her that I would visit on June, 16 during school vacation. Unfortunately, we never met again physically except in a spiritual way.

As the nursing college doors were mercilessly shut at my face, the doors of Vista University were widely opened for me. However, the University didn't offer social work courses and I registered for a degree in education. I obtained good results for the University entrance exam, but I had no registration fees. When I received the University placement letter, my mother and I jumped with joy, as if we could afford it. It was nothing but faith and the love of Christ that gave us courage and motivation. We both knew that there was no money, and the situation was hopeless. My mother's employer, Mr. Mein, told us that he would not be able to help me with study fees. He even discouraged my mother to seek assistance from the bank. He advised me to practice computer in his home every day, and that was the best he could do to help me in my career. Mr. Mein told my mother that it was risky to apply for a study loan for me. He asked my mother who would repay the bank if I die or she dies.

My mother approached her friends and borrowed money from them. They all earned little; however, they all contributed for my registration.

Through the love of God their money covered my registration fees. My total focus into the world of the unseen really worked for me; it turned me as blind as not to realize that the registration fee alone was not enough. I needed accommodation, daily transport and meal fees. One would say I was driven by the power of the Holy Spirit. I had the contact details of one student who was living in Mamelodi; whom I met the day I went to apply for admission at the University. Perhaps it was God's plan, as he always works in His mysterious ways reading the mind of my mother's employer, Mr. Mein, who tried to block my success. God kept his promises and even gave me more than I wished and prayed for. He walked me through to the University. My Heavenly Father never left me until he delivered everything He promised.

I called Keen's family in Mamelodi, and let them know that I was coming. I needed them to help me with accommodation. On my arrival, Keen's mother asked me how much I had for the accommodation, and I told her. She shook her head, and I could read from her face that she was feeling sorry for me. She accommodated me temporarily in her house. Keen's family was a family that might have not been materially well privileged, but they were spiritually rich. It is a family that I personally regard as one of the most powerful instruments that the Lord used to save my life, bring me hope and courage. The kindness I received from Keen's family still reminds me of a scripture from the Hebrews that says "keep on loving each other as brothers and sisters. Don't forget to show hospitality to strangers, for some who have done this have entertained Angels without realizing it". They accommodated me without expecting to be repaid. I still believe that one day they will receive their greatest reward from heaven. God is kind to those who are willing to help the needy and serve Him with all their hearts.

I came to believe by that time, that God's ways and plans about our lives are unique and can never be challenged by anyone. He unlocked all the doors that I thought were locked. In fact, there was no door locked in my life, they were only closed. I was supposed to pull the handles, open, and enter. His thoughts about my life were precious and couldn't be numbered. They outnumbered the grains of sand.

What was impossible with me was possible with him. I always had mental images of what God could do and couldn't do. I always prayed for my future but I never asked Him for what I needed exactly. I needed to go to the university, but instead, I prayed for nursing college entry. God gave me what I needed the most. I prayed wholeheartedly, he listened, and answered and that made me realize the importance of why children should pray, and have a personal relationship with God. My relationship with Him was automatic and unplanned. It is important for parents to introduce children to God, in order to stay protected at all times.

Oudora gave me the ultimate gift of prayer that can never be taken away by anyone. It is a gift that money can't buy in this world. I know that God chose me before I was born. I thank him for making me feel so wonderful and special. Prayer is a spiritual weapon and the armor of God that I will forever put on. It is a treasure that I will carry for the rest of my life. I might have not been brought up with a silver spoon, but God opened all the doors for me. I never had to struggle in life for a long time. Even If I struggled, I overcame the difficulties. He rescued me in time. In my life, each and every single step I took; he was always there to guide me through.

My life was not completely smooth; I went through some illness and challenges at the University. However, the hand of the Almighty kept me safe. He led me with his unfailing love and faithfulness. I never trusted in my own thoughts and wisdom in my studies. I prayed hard every night for my future. He never let me down; for he knew I trusted him with all my heart. In each and everything I did as a child I invited him. He granted me a quiet and peaceful life to feel the joy of the silent world. Living that kind of life and depending totally on the Almighty made me feel like a total stranger in this material world. The only thing I was not aware of was that I had spiritual gifts that drove me to the Zion Christian Church. A Holy place of silence: joy and peace. Zion is one of the biggest churches in South Africa which hold almost half of the population of South Africa. I regard it as a miraculous church of impossibilities; where there is spiritual wisdom, kindness and love. It is a Holy city of peace and harmony.

CHAPTER 2

SECOND CHANCE TO LIVE

No one could narrate how Sibu got consumed by the beauties of the spiritual world, but at least with her mom, Grace, it was easy to relate and understand. When Oudora narrated the story of Grace, her daughter, she said: "one day when she woke up; she noticed that Grace was sleeping for a long time and showed no sign of breathing." Oudora sighed "Unbelievable!" with great shock, she called her "Grace! Grace, Grace . . . ." The child never responded. Oudora trembled with fear, asking herself what might have happened to her little girl Grace. She knew Grace was sick and weak, but never thought she might die any time soon. She tried hard, giving little Grace all types of remedies to make her feel better, but the child's condition deteriorated.

"Grace! Grace, Grace" She called her once more and the child still didn't respond. She touched her body and it was as cold as ice. It seemed as if Grace had passed on. It was good that Oudora was alone in the bedroom; that other children were spared this unusual and terrifying sight. Oudora screamed, cried and said "This isn't really happening, it's just a nightmare." Then, she called neighbors for help, and immediately the elders of the village arrived. As the custom recommends, when someone is suspected to have died, the grannies are called to witness and confirm. When one of the elders arrived, Ms. Latria; she looked at the little girl, touched her like they always did to confirm when someone has passed on. She looked hopelessly at Oudora and nodded, to confirm that the child was gone to the sky families.

"Oh Oudora, there was nothing you could have done to save her, it was time. The Almighty has achieved his will". Oudora was a woman of courage and faith; her heart was as strong as that of a lion. She eventually accepted that Grace was gone. She had a strong faith and knew everything happens for some reason. It was not easy for her to lose her single beloved little girl; however, she remained calm. She made everything to keep herself united for the sake of Grace's spirit to rest in peace. As a Christian, she knew that in every situation we have to be grateful and thankful, pray at all times, for whatever happens is God's will. Oudora did not want to throw away her confidence in the Lord. She was one of the elders of the Catholic Church; who were always there to comfort grieved families, to help them through difficult times, and now it was her turn. This was really a challenge to her; she had to be strong and to shed no tears, so as to prove her faith. As a religious person she didn't have to take out her pain by crying, as she would be considered to have little faith. She had to prove courage and faith by being strong. This was a test that she had to go through. She felt her faith was tested like Abraham, having to give up her single sweet little girl that she loved with all her heart.

As a person who used to serve others; they also came to give their condolence and support. The elders, who were in the bedroom where Grace's corpse was, they slowly and gently wrapped her body with white linen. It was a custom of showing respect to the dead. They believed white sheets will make the spirit of the dead rest in peace. After they finished, they put the corpse on the corner of the bedroom and lit a candle. A candle was meant to lighten up the spiritual path of late Grace as she walked through to heaven.

As the elders were quietly mourning and waiting for the burial, they heard a child sneezing. Out of shock, they frowned and looked at the corner. "It is Grace . . . ." the elders shouted 'She rose up from the dead." The elders rushed to the corner of the bedroom, grabbed her from the floor and quickly uncovered her. Oudora jumped out of joy, calling her little girl "Grace! Grace . . . . !" She couldn't hold her tears, they streamed down her cheeks. "Oh my God, What have I done to deserve your miracle and a wonderful blessing like this one"? People believed that miracles ended with Moses, but it had just happened with Grace. The reason why God gave Grace 'a second chance to live' is still unknown; however, Oudora was grateful and thankful. Her religious life changed a lot; her spiritual bond with God grew more and more.

Oudora's joy was Grace's sadness; she was never happy and isolated herself from other children. Grace was not happy to have been granted the second chance to live. It showed that by the time Oudora and elders were worried and crying about her death; Grace's spirit was having an amazing spiritual tour experiencing the joy of heaven. Her cold body was with them but her spirit was in total tranquility. She was in a land of peace, joy and silence; a place where she felt no hunger, sickness and pain. A distant world of love, kindness and harmony; where there was no hungry mouth to feed. Where the moon and the stars are close, and shine all the time. A place similar to Zion City in Pietersburg (South Africa); where there is no quarrel or sadness. The prevailing silence, love and unity are beyond measure. Grace was angry with God for returning her to earth.

When Grace related her vision, she said "she saw herself with many children of her age. They were singing and praising in a cloudy place, and there was lot of harmony. All the children were jumping with joy and she was among them. Suddenly a powerful hand grabbed her from other children and dropped her down to earth. She heard a terrifying thunder that made her whole body shake with fear." That was the time she sneezed, and woke up with terrible pains all over her body. It took time for little Grace to forgive the Almighty for giving her a second chance to live, as she never wanted to return to this world. She also recalled seeing herself in a place that was naturally covered with green grass and beautiful flowers. She felt peace and faithful love that never ended. There was no pain, sorrow and no suffering. She spent most of her childhood longing to return to the beautiful land of Jerusalem where all the nations meet for eternity. She never considered how grateful and blessed she was to have been given a second chance to live. A chance that many people would die to have. All she needed was to return to the sky families.

Unlike her daughter Sibu, Grace's silence was filled with anger and bitterness of longing to return to the world of the unseen. Sibu's silence was filled with harmony of the joy of heaven. Grace spent most her time in isolation, waiting for God to call her, and it never happened. She waited and listened genuinely with the desire to hear the Great lover, friend and comforter inviting her to the world of harmony. From that time Grace never wanted to live in noisy places. She had a deep longing for the other world and cared less about this land of the living. Her holistic spiritual and emotional healing was not easy. She had a strong feeling that something special was mercilessly taken away from her. She felt as if a part of her had died. Grace felt that she was denied and deprived of her rights to live on the other side of life. For her daughter, Sibu it was completely different, her isolation and loneliness was filled with joyful moments of her friendship with her spiritual imaginary friend "God".

At least for Grace it was understandable why she was different and typically unsociable, and not willing to play with children of her age. For her daughter Sibu it wasn't easy to tell how she got consumed by the unseen world. Was this a spiritual inheritance? "A child would behave or live the same life as her own mother." Maybe to Sibu it was a gift from God, that He called and chosen her among other children as a friend. Sibu was happy and excited to live such a life, but in Graces' eyes one could read bitterness and anger. She was angry with herself and God for bringing her back to life. She loved the spiritual world where she was called, and never wanted to return to the land of the living. Oudora did everything to make her happy; however, nothing could make her daughter happy or satisfied. All she needed was to return to the unseen world. "Mama how did I return to this world" Grace asked Oudora. "I may not know the reasons why the Almighty decided to bring you back to me, and I'm grateful and thankful to have you back" She replied.

Waiting is the most difficult thing to do, yet she had to do it. She had been waiting in vain for her name to be called again to Jerusalem. Instead, she was called to serve the purpose of God at Zion Christian Church. She was called to heal and pray for the sick. The Lord called her to live in his house all the days of her life; delighting in the presence of his perfections and meditating in his temple. She was bitter and angry with God as she believed; God had returned her to suffer in this world of the living. I learned from one of the powerful American Pastors, that God has special gifts for all of us. Grace did not know that God had returned her to life to claim her own amazing prizes; that she was not aware of. She did not know that God had prepared her a table of delights and a feast of all the good things. He had readily prepared her a feast in the presence of her enemies. She was honored to have been given a second chance to live, and her head was anointed with oil. Her cup was waiting and overflowing with blessings. She didn't know that there were neatly wrapped boxes of prizes that were unclaimed. She didn't know that within the post office of heaven there were many gifts of life that were hers.

Gifts have been safely stored in the Heavenly post office shelves. These gifts were even covered with dust, as they had been stored there for a long time. They could only be covered with dust but couldn't be touched by ordinary men. Her name was written on each and every one of them. There were unclaimed cars, children, houses, happy and healthy life, husband and many more. As Grace grew up and accepted Jesus Christ in her heart, her life changed from bitterness to everlasting joy. Her moments of suppression, repression and depression changed into a time of happiness. Her whole life began to overflow with harmony as she started experiencing the joy of Heaven like her daughter Sibu.

Grace lived the abundant life that God meant for her. She worked hard to change people's lives the way she was called by God. She never aligned herself with most of the customs of this world. She was transformed by God into a new person. Perhaps her focus into the unseen world strengthened her personal relationship with God. She was blessed and became like a blessing to Oudora and other people around her. She fruitfully used all the gifts God granted her; ability to prophesy, encourage others, leadership ability and the gift of serving others. Prayer was a family legacy that Grace got from Oudora and it was passed on to Sibu. Prayer was one common thing which united them, and kept them connected to God. Grace left Sibu with Oudora when she was a baby and Oudora transferred all the love she had for Grace to Sibu.

Finally, Grace accepted Jesus Christ and acknowledged her blessings. Ultimately she managed to shut the steel doors of the unseen world and opened the curtains of the future. Maybe Zion Christian Church was a legacy of the family. Grace received emotional and spiritual healing in Zion, to serve the purpose of the Almighty. Later on, God called her to the African Apostolic Churches. The same thing happened with her daughter Sibu. God chose Zion as their spiritual and emotional healing clinic. It was a platform that God had chosen to prepare both of them to be on mission with him. Millions of people, from different countries and Provinces, travel to this African church to find answers about their lives. A Holy place that people never leave with tears, physical pain or shame, for it's a holy place of spiritual wisdom. A place in which there is no sorrow, where the rich and the poor, the black and the white, the able and the disabled live together as one and in harmony. Zion will never teach you how to pray or live for yourself, but how to live an unselfish life and pray for others. I personally regarded it as a blessed place of my Father, where I learned how to live an unselfish life.

CHAPTER 3

AN AMAZING VISION OF "AN EYE AMONG THE STARS"

"Dear Father in the mighty name of Jesus! I humbly come before your throne with all my prayer requests. Dear Father, teach us to appreciate the beauty you have made, and to appreciate all the wonderful and thoughtful creations of nature, Heaven and earth that you carefully created to remind us of your love. At the beginning there was light and the light shone through the darkness with the brightness that an ordinary man couldn't stand.

We may not tell the reasons why you chose us to be the witness of your miraculous revelation tonight; however, we are grateful and thankful, and we will praise you at all times. We perfectly understand that everything in our lives happen for some reason. From this day Lord, help us to believe in you, and to be the witness of this amazing sight. Give us the courage to share this vision with all your children at the time that you will choose. Dear Lord! I perfectly understand that we are nothing and have nothing shiny in this world that will make them believe us; however, we will deliver the message, to those who have ears to listen.

Give us wisdom to recognize and receive you in our lives and above all, grant us the right to become your children. Children who are born not of natural descent: or of human decision or a husband will, but born spiritually out of your will. Thank you for making me, my mother and grandmother feel special among the nations tonight; to be the witnesses of your glory. This is the day you made for us, to rejoice in; and acknowledge that you are the King of kings, Master of all Masters and the creator of Heaven and earth".

Tears slowly welled up her eyes, when she deeply entered into the land of harmony and total surrender. However, she continued with her prayer. "Dear Lord thank you once more, that you chose the three of us to be the witness of this amazing vision, despite our weaknesses and poor background. I now believe that you are the Father of all; the poor and the rich, black and white. For, I know that you have other special children out there that I think deserve your love. Those I heard saying "they are your only chosen children" and I also agree with them Father. For they wear beautiful clothes to church every Sunday, have lot of money and sing beautifully like the birds. It really makes sense Father, when they say "they have inborn privileges and rights to enter heaven". Oh Father! What I admire the most about them is that they travel with their baptismal cards in their pockets and in their handbags. The cards that I'd die to have: The cards that they believe are their entrance tickets to heaven.

Oh Father! What an amazing wise nation! They read the bible every day; they know all the chapters by heart from Genesis to Revelation. They can interpret it with wisdom, they even speak in tongues, isn't it great Lord? Oh Lord, what an amazing blessed nation! I wish I could resemble them. I believe it could have been better that you granted them this opportunity; to witness your miraculous vision tonight, for they really deserve it. What I admire the most about them Father, is that, they look so holy in church. I believe that they behave the same way outside the church; and practice what they preach in their homes. They feed the hungry, give home to the homeless and live according to your ways. Dear Lord I heard them saying Jesus Christ is their only Father. Believe me Father, I envy them so much. I also wish to be a member of Jesus Christ family, just like them, but I learned from them also that it's not easy.

Dear Lord, they even said that if I need to be saved by the blood of Jesus Christ; I have to join their church first. I never thought that to be saved and be covered by the blood of Jesus could be so difficult. Dear Father, I am tempted to join them, but I don't think my grandmother would allow that I move from the Roman Catholic Church to their born again Ministry. Father, I may not know what good they have done to please you; that you granted them the sole rights to be the only ones saved and covered by the blood of Jesus; however, I thank and praise you on their behalf. I believe that one day, my mother, my grandmother, and I will have lot of money to buy baptismal cards and the English bible. So, I could practice by reading it every day. For I need to be like them, and be counted among the blessed children of Jesus Christ.

Forgive me father that I'm talking too much about your few chosen children. It is only that I admire them too much, for they have what I don't have. I have only you, my mother and my grandmother in my life; and the children of Jesus Christ have all the materials of this world in their hands. They even have power to communicate directly with you in tongues. This is your truly blessed nation Father, and I praise you once more for that. I have no doubt that it is for a purpose that I have only you in my life. Baptismal cards may get lost or damaged but your love is endless. Any thief can steal baptismal cards and money, but not your love. Dear Father, I perfectly understand that I'm nothing, and I'm just an innocent Child, but I pray for them for I love them. May your name be praised by their work, for, unlike us, I heard that they never commit any sin!

Dear Father, I honor your decision for choosing them as the only holy ones among all the nations; who will get to enter heaven as they always say. I don't know how they live their daily lives, but I believe that they live a pure Christian life like Jesus Christ. The doors of their homes are forever open; they feed the poor, give water to the thirsty, never gossip or judge. Please Father, teach them how to love and accept us as you have accepted all of us as one. Please guide them to understand that we are all different in this world, and you created that for a reason. For I know in you; Father, that there is no social class, race, color or a special church, you love all your creations equally.

Please, help me become a better educated person, so I could join their beautiful churches; offer lot of money and buy the sole rights of "being born again", and be saved by the blood of Jesus Christ. When that moment comes Father, please help me live a life similar to that of Jesus Christ. According to the bible, Jesus loved and still loves everyone. He never had a class, never boasted of being your single chosen child, and he never belonged to a specific church. He fed the hungry, gave water to the thirsty, and healed the sick irrespective of their health status and economic backgrounds. Dear Lord, I don't mean to be sarcastic, but I have checked through my bible to see the name of the church that Jesus Christ belonged to, but I couldn't see any. Perhaps my granny's bible is old. Dear Father, I don't know if I'm right or wrong, but I have never seen a chapter in my old bible indicating that Jesus Christ ever requested for baptismal cards. It is not mentioned if he ever demanded a special kind of beautiful church uniform either. I never came across a chapter that states that only certain people from certain churches have the sole rights to be his children.

Oh! What a generous son you have, dear Father. He never demanded money from his followers or anyone else. He even gave them food and answered the questions they had about their lives. He blessed and healed them for free and gave everyone life. I wish I could be like him when I grow up. My Heavenly Father, I'm being confused now. Is there one Jesus Christ who belongs to the "born again churches", and another one who belongs to all of us? I mean the son of Mary and Joseph, Jesus Christ, the one that Father Hollanders and Sister Rudy taught me about during Sunday school classes at the Roman Catholic Church? Dear Father, I know that I'm talking and asking too much, but please, consider blessing my family with money, so we could pay for Baptismal cards, and secure better seats in heaven, and in advance. If I could get one, I'll put it in my school bag every day to school, so it will not get lost. Father, I'm sorry, I never told you what happened last Sunday when I visited one of the churches of your beautiful children, those who say they are "born again".

Last Sunday, I visited them and I returned sad. During the offering time, I contributed five cents that my grandmother gave me and it was all she had. I heard the Pastor complaining and mocking. He looked angry and said that he didn't want to see such amounts of money in the offering basket any more. He said those who offer few cents will never receive blessings from you, Father. Dear Lord, I ask for your forgiveness, for I did not know that I was wrong. I only realized thereafter. Believe me Father, I'm not complaining, for I learned that what I did was wrong. I have no doubt that a privileged man of God like Pastor cannot be challenged in any way. He is always right, and above all he is guided by the Holy Spirit at all times. For I believe that he communicates with you all the time. When the Pastor complained I only smiled to gain his favor. I was afraid that one day when you call me or any member of my family to your holy place; we might find him being the door keeper of Heaven and he wouldn't let us in. Dear Father it's really interesting to have Pastors like him; who have already signed up and booked better seats in heaven and in advance, and rub shoulders with great Angels such as Gabriel.

Dear Lord, make us rich so we could contribute more money in church and get the opportunity to receive your blessings. I must admit and confess to you, Father that I envy your chosen blessed children. I used to believe that having a close relationship with you and dedicating my whole life to you was enough, but ever since I had met your blessed children, I started to realize that money makes everything possible in this world. Dear Father, help all your poor children, those who have abandoned fancy church buildings. Your children who couldn't keep up with the standard of fancy clothes, cars, and huge Sunday offerings; some have lost their baptismal cards. Reveal to them that there is still hope. There are other churches out there that will accept them as they are. I'm sorry Lord that I took so long to chat with you. It was really helpful and I even feel spiritually offloaded. I know that my secrets are safe with you. Thanks for being a great listener; a comforter and a kind friend. I pray thee in the name of the Father, the Son and the Holy Spirit Amen". The little girl slowly fell asleep.

I had the feeling that, in that evening, something unusual was going to happen. I felt so spiritually pressured to have a long chat with my Father; and share all my worries with him, so I could be spiritually ready and pure to receive and witness his wonderful miracles. Our Heavenly Father works only in silent places. The night was so brightly beautiful and there was great silence. When I started falling slowly into a deep sleep, I could feel a hand shaking me softly. When I looked up, I saw my mother, Grace. She was dressed in a blue Zion Christian church uniform. She looked so unusual, and beckoned twice without saying a word. I jumped out of my bed and followed her, Oudora also followed her. She led us outside the house right in front of the verandah and asked us to look up in the sky, Wow! I screamed out of joy and excitement! What an amazing sight! We saw a bright kind eye among the stars. The stars were so beautifully crowded surrounding the eye. This eye glimpsed through the darkness. We watched until our eyes were filled with tears of joy.

While I was watching the eye; I felt an inner joy and peace flowing through my heart and mind. Through direct contact with the eye I felt so spiritually connected with my imaginary friend. I felt as safe as never before as if God was up there looking on us in a humble and peaceful way. While we were standing there, exploring this unbelievable sight, Grace started singing a song called "Do you see the light" (A o a le bona lesedi?). I heard that song for the first time. She sang it so beautifully, that we couldn't resist singing with her. The song sounded as if it was one of the Zion Christian church worshiping songs. She even taught us how to dance for it. It was a special kind of beautiful dance; I still cannot forget that song and its dance. Singing that song made me feel so blessed and strongly connected to my Father.

I will treasure and carry this amazing sight in my heart and mind for the rest of my life. All the materials of this world can be taken away from me, but the vision will never be taken away. Water may dry up from the rivers; tears may dry from my eyes, pain may cease to exist, but this vision will stay forever. This vision was probably meant for me only, for reasons only known to God. The strange thing was that the vision seemed to be real to me, but my mother could not recall it the following day though it wasn't a dream. She never ever wanted me to ask her or talk about it again. It happened in live; I wasn't sleeping, and it wasn't a dream. She is the one who woke me up to witness this beautiful sight. The strangest thing to me was; when she called us, she was unusual. Tears were rolling down her cheeks, as if they were flowing from a river. She wasn't herself, perhaps she was filled with the power of the Holy Spirit. Her inner spiritual self was consumed by the power that I believe was of the unseen world. I believe that the moment she called us to witness this sight, she was driven by the power of the Holy Spirit. I have never seen my mother in such a state neither before, nor after that night.

While we were looking up the sky, I felt like something so powerful and great was moving us closer to the eye that was among the stars. I believe that was the power of faith. When I was excited she was only silent and tears kept swelling up from her eyes. Her body was with us, but her spirit and mind were miles and miles away communicating with God. She never stopped weeping; she kept on saying "Yes Lord, thank you Father" every now and then. The sky was filled with gentle kindness from a distance; this was truly an unbelievable sight.

"Oh Father! May this beautiful heavenly vision that you presented to us tonight forever remind us of your covenant. Help us understand that you are our light and salvation, and the stronghold of our lives. During our days of troubles and need, please, be there for us. Never hide your face from us, nor turn away from us in anger. Teach us your ways, and lead us at all times. One thing that we ask and seek from you Father, is to live in your house all the days of our lives. Thanks once more Father for this wonderful vision, we really feel honored tonight Amen."

Praying times were the most joyful moments during my childhood. Prayers enabled me to communicate with my Father, share all my worries and wonderful times. When I had questions; I asked him through prayers, and He answered in visions. When I spoke with him, I felt inner peace and always felt safe for I knew everything I shared with him was safe. I knew that he was not going to tell anybody. The sweetest gift of having God as an imaginary friend was; He knew how to keep secrets. He never judged me, or tried to make me feel bad in any way.

CHAPTER 4

RECEIVING THE MIRACLE OF ZION

I was respected by the elders of the village. I was a child that anyone could easily send on errand without complaining. I was like a mirror that other children could reflect themselves on. Most of them wanted to identify themselves with me. I was more like their role model within the community. Most parents used to scold their children saying that they wish they could behave like me. My focus was more on the spiritual world and helping the elders where there was a need. When I was free after school hours, I spent much time with my grandmother, reading the bible and African folktales. At times, we sang the Roman Catholic songs from the hymn book. I loved singing and it was one of my hobbies. In the afternoons, I attended Gospel choir practice at the nearby church.

Being able to carry the elder's instructions made me the most trusted child within the family, relatives and within the community. My imaginary friend gave me the strength to help where there was a need. He was always there to guide and give me strength at all times. It wasn't like I was totally perfect or supernatural: I was just like all other children. I did complain, but silently in my heart. At times, I cried when I was sent on errand; however, I carried the elder's instructions accordingly. When I was assigned difficult tasks, I would silently call to God, and He would give me the courage and strength to finish in time. Actually, words like "difficult" and "impossible" were not part of my mental vocabulary. God protected me throughout all my childhood and teenage life. He was my light and salvation, and the pillar of my life.

When I was at High school, I started to realize that some of the girls of my Age had boyfriends, and I started to ask my spiritual friend "God" to help me get a stable relationship at the right time. I also realized that it was not easy to get a stable partner by then. However, many boys were attracted by my lifestyle, as I have always been humble, respectful, confident, and distinguished.

One evening, God fulfilled my prayers. I had a vision; I saw myself being happily married to Jones and I was living like a queen. I was driving around with a red car. In the same vision, I was living in a beautiful house in which a little girl appeared one day and gave me a bible, and then she disappeared.

When I woke up I was amazed, and chose not to tell anyone. I was ashamed as I came from a poor family, and I wasn't looking smart. I knew there were other smarter and better educated girls out there who could be part of Jones's life not me. By then, Jones was already doing his second year at the University, and he was studying law. Jane, his sister was in the same class with me, and she was my study partner.

I should not have questioned the power of God, for eventually, my prayers were answered; my dream came true. Jones and I got together, and we had a stable relationship. When everyone celebrated on New Year's Eve counting their blessings, I also counted mine. Our relationship was envied by most of the girls of my home village. At the end of my matriculation year, I obtained outstanding results, and had to move to Johannesburg to my Mom to further my studies.

The following year, I went to Johannesburg leaving my grandmother behind. We said goodbye to each other. My Heavenly Father didn't let me that my grandmother and I were seeing each other for the last time. That was the most painful goodbye of my life. It filled my whole body from the sole of the foot to the head with the pain that had lasted for years. I could not find comfort in anything. I couldn't even enjoy anything at the University, but I completed my studies. Financial problems at the University made the situation get worse. My mother's salary was insufficient to cover for my study fees. She worked hard, struggled to pay for my studies. She even wore shoes with holes under the soles. She was always there for me, but nothing she did could fill the gap of losing my grandmother. Jones couldn't support me financially either, as he was still a student at the University.

I started being ill at the University. I had terrible abdominal pains. My monthly menstrual cycle was completely disturbed. I was examined by many specialists; I went to clinics and hospitals, but none could diagnose my sickness. They kept on telling me that my body was in good health. However, I would feel such a terrible pain that I couldn't walk. I would vomit everything that I consumed to remedy the pains. My illness got so worse that I gave up fighting and decided to die. It never crossed my mind that God is the only one who decides when it is the right time for us to die. Furthermore, I never thought or knew that the demonic spirits were capable of making people sick. I never believed that there were evil spirits and demons in life. I accepted my illness as God's punishment; a punishment whose reason I did not know.

I decided that it was time for me to die and join my Grandmother with all the late families. When Grace noticed that I was getting worse she told me that she had decided to take me to the medical doctor in town; to ask him to give me medication on credit as we had no money. Deep down she knew that I had consulted Doctor Daniel and others several times, and none of their medication made me feel better. We didn't even have money for a taxi to town. We were supposed to walk for almost two hours. The distance was very far based on my condition by then. I refused to go to the Doctor as I was feeling physically exhausted. All I longed for was the eternal healing. I knew that all the physical and emotional pain I had suffered from would come to an end.

I knew I would no longer have to go through hardships in my life. I would no longer feel any pain, and no longer have to walk a long distance to the University with an empty stomach. I knew I would have no more assignments to do, and no lecturers to account to. Everything will come to an end. Physically, I was in extreme pain; but emotionally I felt so relieved and excited. I knew that I would no longer have to wake up early in the morning, and walk eight kilometers everyday from the township to the University; while other students boarded taxis and buses. I knew Maria; my friend at the University would be relieved, as she would no longer need to share her lunchbox with me every day. She wouldn't have to bring me her old clothes, so I could look better like other students. I volunteered everyday at the mini library for the blind children. The library was for those who could not read. I read and recorded CDs and cassettes, because I was offered a cup of tea every day that gave me strength to walk in the afternoon to where I lived. To some students, it was just a mere meaningless cup of tea, but to me, it served as the only meal of strength for the day. These thoughts kept on rolling in my minds and I couldn't stop them. The more they flashed in my mind, the more I cried.

"Sibu! My daughter, I want to take you to the doctor to ask him to give you medication on credit. I think we should walk slowly from Fourways to Bryanston" Grace said. I just looked at her, and I never replied. I couldn't stop tears rolling from my eyes. "Wake up Sibu, my daughter" she asked me again and I said: "Mom I appreciate all your care and support, but I have decided to die, I can't bear this pain anymore, Ma". I closed my eyes as I had no strength to argue with her. My pillow got wet with tears, for I couldn't stand looking at my Mom crying so helplessly, begging me to wake up.

We had no one to help us with transport fares. My father; Matthews, was at home on pension and grace's employers was on vacation. I cried because I believed that nothing could ever heal me. I knew in advance that Dr Daniel would tell me the same thing like before. He would tell me that my womb was fine and in normal position. The pain was so strong that I felt like someone was beating me with a hammer inside my stomach. I could only swallow light food, but not medication.

I only came to realize at a very late stage, that my illness was not a natural one. There were some evil spirits involved. My mother tried many times to advise me to seek help from spiritual healers, and I refused. I believed in God and always thought no evil spirits would attack me. Unfortunately, God does let other things happen to us for many reasons. So we could learn lessons and know that he is God. From my illness I learned that our Father is the Father of impossibilities, and has created all of us for a reason. At last, He sent his Angle of salvation to come to my rescue when all hope was gone; when I was the most hopeless and helpless, and when no Doctor or a nurse could heal me.

Miracles still exist and happen at the right time. One day, a woman called Rachel, an administrator at the University, invited me to the Zion Christian church. She asked me to wear a skirt instead of trousers.

She also asked me to put a hat on, just to cover my head as it was her church practice. I visited the church with her. I couldn't believe what the Holy Spirit revealed to me through the church prophet. He revealed that my illness wasn't a natural one; it was caused by the evil spirits. That's why the medical Doctors couldn't diagnose any physical problem. That explained why I was given different types of medication which never helped improve my condition.

Unbelievable! The Priest gave me some water to drink and the prophet told me that on the seventh day I will receive my healing. I had some doubts on how simple water from the tap could heal me. Especially after specialists had tried their best, but failed. The only difference was that the Priest blessed the water. I'm not asking anyone to believe me, for I have nothing to gain. On the third day, the miracle happened; I was completely healed beyond reasonable doubt. The miracle I have been waiting for, for years. The seventh day was too far. Everything happened fast, and I wished my granny had still been alive to witness the greatness and power of the Almighty. I completed my studies, got permanently employed, got married to Jones, and we were blessed with a baby boy, called Tshedimosetso.

CHAPTER 5

ABANDONING MY IMAGINARY FRIEND

I got married and my total focus moved from the silent world of the unseen into the noisy material world. I couldn't resist the temptations of the devil. I forgot all about God and prayers. I don't recall kneeling down and thanking God for his blessings any day during my happy marriage. I took a break from prayer and from the spiritual world. My relationship with God and our spiritual bond got broken. I established new bonds with my husband and the in laws.

I put all my trust on my beloved husband. All I cared about was; my husband, my son, my house, my cars, my money. Those were the only things that I was concerned about. I used to go shopping almost every day. My husband Jones was my only worry and my pillar of strength. I forgot the hand that fed and protected me throughout my childhood until I had completed University studies. I completely forgot about my imaginary friend who had always been there for me since I was a child. It was surprising how easy I was consumed by the riches of this world. I never tried to maintain balance between the spiritual and the material world.

I cared less about my own parents and relatives, and they visited me rarely. I never had a bible and never thought of having any. I never bothered myself reading spiritual books. The poor, the needy and community work were none of my business. My parents were alive and loved me so much, but I never worried visiting or buying them groceries. I lived like a queen, driving the expensive cars of that time. The community in which I lived in respected me a lot. I was a teacher, and my husband was a senior prosecutor. Going to church became none of my worries. I attended the church only on days when I was not busy. Sundays were my best days to show off how delicious I could cook. I prepared all kinds of delicious dishes, and at times would try new recipes to impress my in-laws and my friends. My husband and I were highly respected in our area. Jones never attended the church, but at least he believed in God. He was too politically critical about the church practices. The last time he attended the church was when our son, Tshedimosetso was being baptized.

My whole life was covered with the veil of darkness. I was so blind and couldn't even notice that I wasn't walking on the right path. I thought it was fine and I was on the right track. It's only now that I realize I was living a dangerous and unsafe life, and I was vulnerable. However, God covered me with his hand safely. He had probably reflected on those prayers that I used to say when I was a child; as they were all meant for the future to cover for days when I would not be able to pray. I prayed God for: good health, education, and happy marriage. He delivered and after that I completely forgot everything He had done for me. I felt that I was strong enough to stand up on my own. I relied too much on my own strength, understanding, wisdom, and abilities. Jones was my source of strength and advice. I never asked God for guidance. My in laws and friends were my advisors; I turned to them when I needed help or some motivation.

I turned my back on God, and forgot all my promises to him, but He never abandoned me. He kept me safe, strengthened me, and held me with his hand. One weekend, I decided to accompany my brother in law and his wife to the Zion Christian Church, in Pieterburg. My brother in law, Stones was a Priest at the Zion Church. When we arrived at the church, a prophet revealed to me that the Holy Spirit says: "my marriage and my happy life would come to an end, and that God will take away all he blessed me with. For He brought me to this world to serve his purpose, but I am living my own selfish life. My purpose was to heal and pray for the sick and the needy". He sent me to this world: "to change lives, give hope to the hopeless, and help the helpless". He said that God would take away all my possessions including my family so as to make me aware of the fact that "He is God and there is none like him". The man told me that God had called me to the Zion Christian Church for the unique reason of serving his purpose.

The prophet left without saying a word after delivering the message to me. I started to question what he said in my mind. I paid little attention to his words and even undermined him. I was convinced he made up all those stories to scare and persuade me to join the Zion Christian Church. I never believed in things that were revealed by the Holy Spirit to me. My arrogance was greater than anything else. I even asked myself several times who that man could be, coming out of nowhere and telling me that God was going to let my marriage break apart. The fact that my life was filled with happiness and wealth made me believe that nothing bad could happen.

One night, a simple phone call from my beloved and trustful husband changed my whole life. Jones called and said: "Sibu, I'm sorry I won't be able to be part of your life any longer". The tears swelled from my eyes for the whole night. I couldn't do anything to stop them. In the morning when I woke up, life wasn't the same anymore. Everything had changed overnight. The whole world had turned upside down. I felt like falling down into an endless dark and empty hole; even a blind man could feel it was dark. Deep dark clouds of sorrow covered me up. People who used to live with me before could not recognize me anymore. I became the mockery and the laughing stock of Lichtenburg area. I moved from riches to rags. I had to struggle to raise my kids. Financial problems made the situation get worse. Lawyer's letters kept coming in every month, and court sheriffs became part of my life. I remember jokingly calling the Lawyers that handled my accounts "my uncles" as I was handed to them by stores that I couldn't pay. I used to call them Uncle Norman, uncle Liberty, Uncle Jean and J etc. That was the only way to deal positively with the financial constraints.

Every day I received phone calls from different stores and lawyers demanding payment. I had a special tact to deal with them. When they called on the fifteenth of the month, I told them I would pay on the thirty first. On the thirty first when they called; I would promise to pay on the seventh. From the seventh it would be the fifteenth, and from the fifteenth the next date. It became a vicious circle. That was the only way I found to deal with the pressure. Initially, I was wholly dependent on my husband, as he had a good job. We both had our own family debts, and shared responsibilities within the household. He left me alone in serious debts and in the middle of nowhere, and never looked back. Life became hard for me; however, I never gave up. I had to find strength in the Lord and take him as my pillar of hope.

The pain of loss was so terrible that sometimes; I had to drive from work to home during lunch time to go and pray God for strength. At times, I had to isolate myself from my colleagues and have a short prayer for strength at work. None of them could notice that. I would smile at them while my heart was being torn apart. I had to pretend I was happy for the sake of reducing further humiliations and unnecessary gossips. I knew that as soon as they saw me crying they would have something to talk about. The emotional pain weighed on my spirit and I felt torn apart inside. I cried alone and prayed God to give me courage to deal with the situation. The pain was so strong that I never thought it would heal. Slowly it went away through prayers and encouragement from the Zion Christian Church. I became stronger and stronger every day, and started accepting my unfortunate situation. This was more like a bomb that came out of nowhere and destroyed my whole happiness. My kids were the sweetest thing that gave me reasons for fighting hard to survive. I had to be strong for them, for my parents, and relatives.

Every single day was filled with pain. A pain that I thought would never end. Sometimes, I would stay alone in my bedroom, cry helplessly asking God why He did let that happen to me; Why He didn't give me a second chance. I doubted if He was listening or if He really cared. I remember both my friends, Spongy and Bells, comforting me that the pain would come to an end, and heal eventually, which I never believed, for I was convinced that I would suffer from that disappointment for the rest of my life.

"Oh, what a shameful man Jones is! Abandoning a woman in such conditions; we are really sorry Sibu. Don't despair though, everything gonna be alright". Those are the words I used to hear from people in my community. At times, I could feel it in my heart that their words of comfort weren't genuine. In a small community like Lichtenburg bad news travels very fast. I once met an old colleague with his wife whom I've never met before. When he greeted me, his wife asked if I was Sibu, and I said yes, but I was curious about why she asked me such a question. She bluntly let me know that people had been gossiping about me at her office almost every day. That made me realize that I was the talk of the town, and I hated Lichtenburg more. I got fed up, and I wanted to move out of Lichtenburg. I applied for different jobs at different places. I tried everything to get money and leave the area, but none of my plans succeeded. As time went on I started to accept that God had a unique plan about my life. Being unable to move out of Lichtenburg in spite of the challenges forced me to surrender totally and put my whole life into God's hands. I decided to be patient and serve the purpose of the Lord with all my heart.

I started to realize that people didn't love me; they loved what I possessed. The material world deserted me. If mobile phones and walls around people's homes and offices had been able to talk by then; they would have told me that they had been tired of hearing people gossiping about my name. Never ever count on people of this material world to support you in hard times. Lean upon the promise and strength of God. When my whole life was falling apart, when there was no one to talk to, I returned to where I belonged. I returned to the world of the unseen and to my imaginary friend. However, I had lost all his contact details during the busy times of my happy days. I had to start a new journey and seek him first. I gave up my selfish life and God welcomed me back, but life wasn't the same anymore. I had to work hard to regain God's trust and reclaim my position within the spiritual world.

When I was overwhelmed with pain and sorrow, I turned to the Zion Christian Church for help. Finally, I surrendered and joined the Zion Christian Church. The day I went for baptism at Magaliesburg, I was crying. I cried for the whole Sunday, for the emotional pain I had was double the physical pain—the pain of losing my family and the pain of seeing people isolating themselves from me. Personally I was not in favor of the Zion church. I only went there for God's sake, and to serve his purpose.

When other new members were rejoicing on the baptismal day for being born again, I only cried. I had never planned to be a Zion Christian Church's member, or join any of the born again Ministries. I had never been in favor of these churches because of their strict practices and high commitment in church. The reason being that I knew I wasn't perfect, and didn't want to bind myself with any rules of this world before God that I might fail to keep, due to many temptations. I never wanted to do anything that will upset God. I don't mean to be judgmental, but I have seen people entering into covenant with God in many churches, but at the ultimate end they failed. Unfortunately, in my life experience, I learned that God doesn't entertain words like "I don't want, or I don't like" God's plan about my life were totally different from my own. He included Zion Christian Church in his plan about my life; my duty was to adhere to his plan. I had no choice but to do what God wanted. Being part of Zion Christian Church made people to isolate themselves more from me. However, I cared less, for I knew my Heavenly Father sent me there for some reason.

It wasn't their place to decide about my life, and I didn't need their approval either. Even though I cared less about what people used to say, I kept on asking God why he had called me to Zion. I also didn't understand why he had sent me there. Every time when my mind was filled with "why questions" within the church, God would send his prophets to tell me not to worry. He kept on promising me that He was watching over me, and I was there for a purpose. I never got money, silver, diamond, or Gold from the Zion Christian Church, but it groomed me into an industrious, spiritually strong, and young dynamic woman. I learned the wisdom and the joy of praying. I was empowered with the knowledge and wisdom to establish a strong relationship with God. Eventually, the pain disappeared. I had lot of support from the church and regained my initial link within the world of the unseen.

I regained my old self and regained my spiritual and personal relationship with God. Every day I prayed as if it was my last day. I had to search for a long lost imaginary friend. My search was through daily prayers, and Zion helped me to trace my long lost spiritual friend. Finally, we got connected in a special spiritual way, and the connection was much stronger than never before. I started to change from calling Him my imaginary friend, and I called him "Father".

I then started to accept and move on with my life. I got transformed into a humble and self respecting young woman. I was always there to assist where there was a need. The teachings of Bishop and his priests gave me courage and strength to live. I became dependent on God and not on my own understanding and wisdom. When there was no food in my house, I kneeled down and ask God. When I faced challenges, I prayed for his deliverance, and never depended a lot on people.

I got the spiritual keys to open all doors through prayers. Zion might not have given me gold, but it had enabled me to get fully connected to the world of the unseen, and live a golden life. I was never given diamond or all the richness of this material world, but I stayed physically healthy and spiritually alert. There was a price to pay when I gave up all my life to God: I had to pay by serving the community, by giving myself to be used by the Lord, loving my neighbors, and lastly praying all the time. The sweetest thing about Zion Christian Church is that members were required to commit themselves to the Lord and not to the church. Basically, I lived a life that was purpose driven and full of spiritual freedom.

We were taught to pray hard not for ourselves but for others. We had sleepless weekends gathering at night vigils praying for those in hospitals, prisons, and other situations. We prayed for other problems affecting the whole world. That was the easiest thing to do for me. I paid by giving myself completely unto the Lord. It wasn't because I wanted to please the priests or wanted a position in the church, but because I loved my God. I will love and respect the Zion Christian church for all the days of my life. Nothing and no one will ever make me forget Zion, for it is my home. Even though my Heavenly Father asked me to move from Zion, and establish His ministry of St' Mary, spiritually I'll keep in touch, for it saved and changed my life in a way that words cannot explain. I will forever stay connected, for I believe it's my home of courage, wisdom, and strength.

I started to live an unselfish life. I served the community I lived in; with all my heart, helping the needy and praying for the sick. At times, I followed the Bishop of Zion wherever he was sent by God to pray for the nations. He was invited most of the time in many provinces and countries for praying. His teachings became my treasures and the instruments that I used to fight spiritual warfare. The peace and joy I felt by then cannot be compared to anything money could buy.

I might be nothing and not be able to speak in tongues, or move the mountains through prayers; but I will whisper the name of Zion in all my prayers. It's through Zion that I regained my strength and hope after a traumatic family breakup. It is through Zion that I got healed when I was hopeless and helpless. I got healed when I was about to give up on life; when there was no medical or spiritual doctor or nurse to heal me from teenage abdominal pains. One day, God made his promise to me that I shouldn't panic or give up on Him in any way, for one day I will be free from all the financial constraints and difficulties.

God made a promise that my whole life was going to change for the best. He told me that He called me to Zion to prepare me for more tasks to come in the future. He also said that one day the nation would be amazed by the way the Holy Spirit will use me. He would use me to change lives, and the nations would praise Him by my work. In addition, the Lord said through faith and serving the community, I would be promoted at work. I would secure funds from the Government and other private organizations for the unemployed youth, the underprivileged children, and their families. Through my prayers many people would be healed. If I kept on helping the needy and helpless, I would be called overseas one day and end up being in the parliament. To confirm that, the prophet who delivered the message asked me to go to the higher Priests offices, to record God's promises in the church books at the Head Quarters, because one day I would return to the church and give thanks to God.

Honestly I was not excited, and I had some doubts. I didn't believe that so many blessing would be granted to me. By that time the situation looked hopeless. After five years, he delivered all his promises. I established the organization to help unemployed youth in my community, children living on the streets, and those from disadvantaged families. Fortunately, the organization received financial support from overseas and from the government. It wasn't much, but the funds kept the organization sustainable.

The following year I was nominated as the best teacher in my Area in the National Teachers' Awards. I was promoted at work as head of department, and awarded a scholarship to the United States of America to further my studies. He delivered all his promises, and that made me realize that when we serve the Lord with all our heart, He delivers.

CHAPTER 6

THE JOY OF
ZION UNVEILED

I may have been called by the Almighty to move from the Zion Christian Church to St. Mary's Inter denomination Ministry, but Zion will forever be my home. I will remember it with good memories and with tears of joy. I will never stop talking about the greatness of the Almighty and his mercy for saving my life by calling me to Zion, my Father's land. A land of peace and silence where every woman is my mother and every man is my father. There are no tears, no pain, or shame in my Father's land of Zion. An African promised land which overflows with honey and milk.

People always say miracles ended with Moses, but not in Zion. A place where there is nothing impossible. A spiritual land and a home that my ancestors fought so hard for, so we could live in it and forever rejoice. They were engaged in spiritual warfare. They suffered and sacrificed their own personal needs and desires. They fasted and went to bed with empty stomachs for many days, praying to God so we could have spiritual connection to the unseen world. They went through troubles and frustrations so we could live. They were attacked by the evil forces but never despaired. They sustained serious criticism from our neighbor African church sisters and brothers but never gave up.

The ancestors and the founders of Zion sacrificed their own happiness. They prayed for us, so we could have this beautiful land today.

Wake up child of Zion; for the nations are coming to seize your beautiful land. Stand up! Light up your lamp so the Almighty will never give you unto the desire of your enemies. The nations will rise up against you to conquer your mountain of Zion. The nations are closely watching over the greatest prophet of Africa. They will take him away from you, and you will have no one to turn to or wipe your tears. He is the greatest Angel of Africa: an Angel of hope, healing, wisdom, and courage. He never judges nor criticizes. When our former president Dr. Nelson Mandela fought and suffered for our economic, social, and personal freedom; the Wise one of Zion fought for our spiritual freedom.

Wake up child of Zion; wipe all those tears from your eyes, for the time is coming where you shall have to share your land with the upcoming nations and generations of this world. You will become like strangers and beggars in your own homeland. God sent the Greatest Prophet of Zion to Africa to pray for all of us; that is why the nations are coming to him from different countries and overseas to seek wisdom.

The founders and the late kings of Zion spent sleepless nights praying for the generation's health, success, safety, and freedom. Today we are a blessed and prosperous nation because of their prayers, but some children of Zion have forgotten. From the king of Zion I learned nothing but an unselfish prayer. A spiritual weapon that I will forever use and treasure for the rest of my life. Zion enabled me to be spiritually connected to my Heavenly father. Indeed, Zion is a land of courage, bravery, and wisdom. It is through the King of Zion that I learned to wake up at night, leave my own comfortable duvets sets, kneel down, and pray not for myself, but for all other nations. It is through him that

I learned that in God there is no color, no race, and no class. We are all the same. I would be a fool if I could fail to stand up before the nations and declare the greatness of my Father of Zion.

God revealed to me several times when I was in Zion that "My child, I called you to Zion for a reason, and I, your Heavenly Father will never reveal your purpose in this church until you are ready". I never understood when the Lord said that my purpose was the greatest. I lived in Zion with emptiness. I tried hard to search for meaning about my life and my purpose, and nothing was revealed. I waited until God was satisfied with my spiritual level. I consulted with many church prophets, but the Lord kept it unrevealed. I followed the bishop of Zion wherever he was called to pray. I followed him to different provinces and countries trying to search for meaning and my purpose, but my Heavenly Father just remained silent.

One day, I visited one of the Zion Church branches in Zeerust, where many people gathered for praying and healing. The Priest in that area was believed to be spiritually powerful. Many people got healed through his prayers. I needed his help to pray and save the life of an innocent eight year old girl; who was totally consumed by the evil forces of the unseen world. She was feared by people. I had to risk my life and fight for her salvation; for I knew that the Lord was my light and salvation. He was the stronghold of my life and I wasn't to fear anything. I drove a long distance with the little girl to Zeerust. I could read from the faces of my local church priest that they wished to help her; however, they were afraid and uncomfortable to come close to her.

When I approached the Priest in Zeerust, he looked at me, smiled and said: "my child, do you see many people gathered here today" I said: "yes Sir" and he said, "God says, He brought you to life to pray for and heal the nations. You are supposed to be in a place like this: People coming to you for prayers". He further interpreted the message of God by saying that my purpose in life was the same as his, but since I am a woman in the Zion church I would not be allowed to serve the purpose of God the way he was doing it. The Church had some restrictions on women regarding the healing process and ministry.

I couldn't understand why the Priest said my calling was the same as his. He never ended the conversation, and I also never bothered him asking further questions. I didn't even believe in what he said. I knew that women could only be prophets in Zion under serious restrictions and only if it was their spiritual calling. In my own thoughts I believed God might have made a mistake by giving me the spiritual gifts to heal, as I was a woman in Zion, and it wasn't possible. By that time, I never thought of the possibility that God might ask me to move to another Ministry where I would be able to serve his purpose.

I heard some people saying that Zion was the best church of God. He called us to be there forever. If we move out of Zion to other churches we would die or become mad, and that wasn't true. I was strongly convinced that the Priest of Zeerust didn't mean what he said about my calling. He might have been confused, but somehow I had questions rolling in my mind about visions I had most of the time. I saw myself being part of women elders in church who were in leadership, but I never understood those visions. I knew that no ordinary woman like me would become a leader within the Zion Church.

The highest priests were the only ones who could decide and choose the women to be in church leadership. The women in my visions were more like women priests. They were identified with the sign of the tears; women of this particular section in church are meant to wipe the tears of all the people who are in pain and need help within and outside the church. At times, I was troubled by visions in which I saw women of all races coming to me crying for help. I saw white women among them crying and not saying anything. Their eyes were full of tears. I couldn't interpret those visions. It's only later that I realized that God was revealing to me that I was part of the church women leaders in a spiritual way, but I couldn't understand by then.

Some of the duties of women on church leadership were to perform certain healing tasks to other women, youth, and children. What amazed me the most was that when God sent His prophets to deliver messages of the church; I was called together with other women on leadership to receive his message? It was something that happened rarely with young women of my age. At times I felt so uncomfortable to see myself among those women because I was only a young woman, and I wasn't part of them in leadership. The messages that the Lord revealed were based on church leadership matters.

At times, I could see that they were not happy, but there was nothing they could do; for the fact that God was working in His mysterious ways and they couldn't challenge his ways. Sometimes, I thought God had made a mistake by including me in the group of church women leaders; to receive his messages of deliverance and guidance, and on how they were to intercede for others. That was a spiritual challenge to me. I did as the Holy Spirit guided me, I prayed part of the time for all nations, and spent sleepless nights interceding, the other part.

Situations like that brought lot of confusion into my life. For I didn't understand why God gave me a special treatment as the leaders; for the fact that I was nothing within the church, and I knew I would never be anything. I never wanted anything to do with church positions and leadership in my life. I believed that they would not add any value to my life. I still don't understand why Christians are fighting for church positions; to me, it doesn't make any sense. Why would I struggle and sweat for church positions with no salary. All I need is my personal relationship with God, serving the community, and changing lives. I would rather fight hard and spend sleepless nights praying to gain more spiritual wisdom and power; so I could change lives and give people answers about their lives. I would do anything to win the love of God rather than fighting for recognition and power within the church.

People might not agree with me, but I think it's better to sweat for the community, and serve the helpless people who will appreciate your efforts rather than serving the people in the church, who might criticize, judge, and never appreciate your efforts. Serving the community was the only place where I felt at home and appreciated. After helping the people through God's guidance, I always felt an inner joy and victory. I felt like I had shared something special with members of the community.

When I was in Zion, I enjoyed serving the community outside the church. My passion for serving the community was spurred by the prophetic massages that I received most of the time. God wanted me to help his children at all times and share with the needy, even if it meant giving my last piece of bread. He provided at all times.

People who knew me in Zion criticized me a lot. They felt that I was overdoing the community work, and I was too much committed to church. I travelled most of the time to different places on weekends to pray, and to where Bishop was called. They felt that I was wasting money and petrol, because they didn't understand. They didn't know that I wasn't doing that out of pleasure. I was guided by the Holy Spirit. However, I never told anyone the reasons behind my commitment. I don't mean to be judgmental, but people I knew within the church never served the community. They only cared about their own personal desires and families.

One day, when I was voluntarily serving as a guidance counselor; I came across a little girl who was possessed by the demonic spirits. I received lot of criticisms from people. They told me to leave the eight year old child alone so to avoid danger. Yes! I must admit they had a point, but I couldn't stand watching a child's future being destroyed by the force of darkness, while it was in my powers to pray for her deliverance. That child was totally consumed by the darkness world. She was brave and proud of herself. Everyone kept their distance from her. They were terrified and feared for their lives. I tried to involve the social workers, psychologists, and local priests. All of them came only once and never returned because of fear. She related her story innocently, proudly, and confidently to everyone: She demonstrated her satanic powers with bravery, not knowing that she was a danger to the society. She was proud of having special powers that nobody had.

People were so afraid of telling her that her evil powers were a danger to them; they only kept quiet and listened to her. Perhaps they were afraid because we never had incidents like that before in our area; children of her age possessing such powers. They were afraid that she might attack them. The only time we heard of those incidents it was on movies, radios, televisions, and from books. One woman advised me to take the child to Zeerust, and I did.

The name of the little girl was Hope. From my communication with her I learned that she was introduced to Satanism by an old woman who was a neighbor to her. An old woman who looked after her most of the time when her father was away: In my own opinion, I think the old woman got tired of giving the little girl food all the time. She then introduced her to the world of darkness, so she could be empowered with the skill of stealing food and other things for herself. Hope mentioned that she used to drink peoples' blood. She also indicated that she flew at night to people's houses, to steal food such as sugar, rice, corn meal, and other foods.

Hope's main task was to collect food from the houses of weak people at night. People who never prayed in their homes were easy targets for her. That explains why parents in most families complained that children consumed a lot of food. From that time I learned that parents had been blaming their children for things they had never done. Some parents complained that groceries couldn't last until the end of the month. Parents were not aware that some of their groceries were being stolen at night by people of darkness.

Hope reminded me of my mother's vision that she shared with me. God revealed to her that we are all like candles on earth. People who pray hard are represented within the spiritual world as burning candles. Those who do not pray are like candles that do not burn. The lights shine in the houses of those who pray hard, with the brightness that Angels cannot ignore. Their brightness attracts the Angels from heaven who come to protect them. As a result, the evil forces of darkness never go near them. To those who are less committed they are like dim candles. For those who never pray, their houses are always dark and their homes are easy access platforms for the demons. Those were the houses that Hope explained to me that were the easiest to enter, and she could steal food from them.

I learned a lot from Hope, as she had more experience within the world of darkness. She further explained that she used people who were not spiritually strong and never prayed, when she needed some food from houses which she couldn't easily enter. She captured their spirits at night and sent them to houses of people where she was afraid of getting into. That explained why some people woke up in the morning being exhausted. It's because their souls never had rest at night. Their bodies were in bed, but they were spiritually on duty in the dark world. We could only be safe, and avoid being instruments of dark forces by praying. If we establish a strong relationship with God, we will be saved also. Praying makes our spiritual lights shine forever, repel the evil forces, and attract Heavenly Angels.

I may not understand the reasons why God sent Hope to my life, while I was a member of the Zion Christian Church family; however, I was grateful and thankful. She was a little girl, but I learned a lot from her. She was one of the most powerful instruments that God used to urge me to move spiritually, and acknowledge my spiritual gifts. It is through Hope that I came to realize that the Priest in Zeerust was right about my mission. Another famous prophet and a Radio preacher, Pastor OJ, also revealed to me that my purpose in life was to pray for people and deliver message of hope and salvation; he told me that the first time I met him as he came to pray for the little girl. Hope's life experiences urged me to research more on the world of darkness. All her satanic experiences were the same as those I read about from American religious writers.

I heard about lots of negative stories about Zion Christian Church, and it is not my place to defend the church, or convince anyone somehow, for I have nothing to gain. However, I feel partly compelled to share my own wonderful experiences and the joy I felt within the church. I want to thank my Heavenly Father that He introduced me to the large family of Zion Christian Church. It was truly an experiential journey full of joy and amazing experiences. I still agree that Zion is not an easy church to understand, especially when looking from a distance. I joined Zion with uncertainty and a lot of curiosity. I was not happy and I was angry with God at first for sending me there, but at the end, I was the most grateful and thankful.

I will remember my days in Zion Church with a smile. I was always smart with my scarves that matched my clothes and shoes. I remember that the time I joined, I did not have any skirts or trousers, which were recommended for women, as part of church practice. I went for shopping and I bought the most beautiful skirts, jackets, dresses, scarves, and matching earrings. My skirts were long enough to cover my knees. Many young women around my community got encouraged by the way I looked like. People were stereotyped about the church, since it was an African church. They said women in Zion were not smart and were untidy, and that was not true.

I did everything in my powers to find joy, happiness, and silence in Zion. Some elders within the church weren't happy about the way I dressed. I think they might have been overpowered by some jealousy, and for the fact that the church was in the rural area. They believed that women had to wear long dresses, no high heel shoes and no earrings. At times, they gathered in small groups to talk about me, but they never approached me to express their dissatisfaction about my attire, and I could read it from their faces. Youth admired the way in which I dressed. The women church leaders didn't want to accept that the bishop ruled out that everyone in Zion should look after themselves, and look smart at all times. I will never stop to admire the way in which the women choirs of Sannishof, Klerksdorp, Soweto, Alexandra, and Moria sang. They were very smart and sang so beautifully. The standard of Zion music within those choirs was very high. They looked exceptionally well, neatly and beautifully dressed up in their church uniform, and some in their own home attire.

I will always miss the highest standard of the music of the female church choir in Moria at Pietersburg. Their sweet melodic voices made me shed tears of admiration and joy. I admired the choir conductor; she was outstanding. I felt that I was so unfortunate to have been residing far from those areas and being part of the choirs in Lichtenburg. I couldn't find joy in the standard of music in my area. During choir practice I felt like running away from the church. Sometimes when it was time to attend the choir practice I got filled with anger. I felt like I was in a total strange world, and that made me cry when I was alone. I asked God why He wanted me to sing in the female choir, and he never answered. I was frustrated by the fact that other choirs from other Provinces had an outstanding standard of music. In my area, the standard was very low. There was no one to confront the choir conductors to change the music, and the members seemed to be happy and proud of that type of music. Maybe I was the only one who couldn't enjoy their music. People from the community criticized the female choir a lot and there was nothing I could do, they might have been right. Sundays in Lichtenburg churches were enjoyable, the music was good, and the majority of the members attended: men, women, youth, and children. The priests did everything to make everyone find meaning and enjoyment within the church.

When I was still a member of Zion, everyone paid for their own family funeral plans at the end of every month. The money was deposited at the bank. Funeral claims were done at one of the reputable insurance companies. There was no way that Bishop or the priests could have used our money for their own benefits as people were saying. We were criticized by other neighboring churches that we gave all our money to the church. I was never bothered by all those criticisms because I knew they weren't telling the truth. This was one of the reasons why

Zion Christian church is attended by almost half of South Africans. It is because all the members are encouraged to pay for their funeral plans only. There is no tithe or huge Sunday offerings required. Most of the families who couldn't keep up with the financial demands from the born again churches and other Missionary churches eventually joined Zion Christian Church. The spiritual prophesy and healing is free.

I travelled to areas where bishop was invited by the government to pray and preach. He addressed crime prevention, economic empowerment, poverty alleviation, family violence, and other health issues. He encouraged members to live peacefully with their neighbors and support them in times of need. He preached the message of hope and peace, and further encouraged members to pray to God at all times, to read the Bible, and to respect and love one another and their neighbors. I took all his words of wisdom and made them part of my life.

I will carry and treasure the peace and silence which I enjoyed at the Headquarters of Zion in Moria whenever I visited. All the people were equally treated. There were no criticisms and no humiliations; we lived happily together as one. I wished it had not been far from Lichtenburg where I lived. In Zion, people's needs are met. What I liked the most was that God would warn me in time anytime I had to face trouble, and I would pray for protection. Those who ignore prophetic messages end up in trouble.

CHAPTER 7

THE EAGLE VISION

Visions exist and have important messages about our lives. Every person in this world is represented by a guardian angel, spirit guard, or an ancestor in the spiritual world. It depends on different religious beliefs of people. People call them differently; however, we are all represented by our guardian Angels in a special and spiritual way. People who are exposed to the spiritual world of the unseen such as Psychic mediums, spiritual healers, prophets, and traditional healers will agree with me in this regard. It is our faith that keeps us strongly represented and connected to the spiritual world and to God.

Our faith, beliefs, and prayers make our spirit guards to be strong, and to represent us well within the spiritual world. Once we pray hard we give our spirit guards power to connect us to the spiritual world. This differs from different cultures and religions. Spirit guards are strongly connected to God through our faith and prayers. Many people have personally seen Angels appearing to them in visions. Some have dreamed their own late brothers, sisters, parents, grandparents, or relatives telling them of the good or bad things to come. Many people have dreamed their late families warning them of danger to come, and it happened exactly as they said. Visions serve as a way of communicating God's messages. They also reveal our future and his plans about our lives. Some visions are our ultimate treasures and gifts, which we may not easily forget and have special meaning in our lives.

The more we pray and try to be spiritually pure, the more our spirit guards get power to watch over us, and keep us alert through God's power. There are some individuals and religious groups who believe that people who passed away are demons. I have met some Christians particularly the 'born again', saying that all the late people who appear in our dreams are demons, and I personally disagreed with them. I don't think my late Grandmother is a demon. We used to live peacefully together and we loved each other so much. She taught me how to pray to God, serve the community and love others. I once asked my close friend who was a born again, after her mother's death if she believed that her mother has turned into a demon, and she kept quiet. Several times after my granny passed on, she appeared in my visions and she taught me how to pray to God and how to pray for others. She even gave me bible verses which includes Psalms 27, she advised me to use my rosary at all times. She interpreted Psalm 27 and further taught me that it was my pillar of strength. She advised me to read it all the time and pray thereafter. She told me to pray when I feel lonely, troubled, or in need of guidance. She explained to me that when I pray I should pray to God and not to her. I liked one Priest when he was praying, he would say: "may our late ones be counted among the Saints of Heaven and enjoy the resurrection." That convinced me further that not all the dead people are demons.

If I had wings like an eagle, I would fly high and go to a place where no ordinary man could see or reach me. So I could be able to serve my Heavenly Father with peace. Where there are no criticisms and where everyone is equal. A place free of noise and destructions; where nothing will block my ears. The more we humiliate, judge, and hurt one another's feelings, the less we become spiritually connected. Feelings of rage, anger, and jealousy are not needed within the spiritual world. Negative thoughts and feelings drive our guardian Angels far away from us.

Knowing all the bible verses by heart doesn't automatically make people spiritually connected to God. For people to grow spiritually, they have to live a life that is spiritually clean and pure. They have to avoid emotional pain and serious mental disturbances. Once there is silence and purity within their minds, then they will be able to hear God's voice. Our Heavenly Father would like to talk to all of us, not to certain people only. There is no better person or church; to God, we are all his children. We should limit our criticisms and judgments, avoid situations which might cause us or others pain and frustrations.

Everyone is a spiritual eagle of God, and He has granted all of us wings to fly. When we fly high up in the sky, we will not have to receive traffic tickets like when we drive on normal routes. We will not be exposed to accidents or any troubles. We will be able to notice danger from a distance and avoid it. We will fly high and have no powerful laws imposed on us by any one. When we acknowledge our eagle blood and fly, we will only be governed by rules not written by natural or normal ink. We will be guided by the spiritual will of God.

Eagles of God have no time to judge; they do not even notice when their bank accounts are empty. They are always happy and have unique ways of dealing with challenges. They have a clear vision and see things from a distance. Eagles talk less and listen most of the time. Eagles are the Prophets of God and I believe every one is a prophet. Eagles never share their problems with friends for there is nothing to talk about. They share all their frustration and challenges with God. They are the messengers of God and have been assigned a responsibility by God to pray for others. All church leaders are eagles and have the responsibility to represent their congregations within the Heavenly parliament. The Heavenly parliament setting is almost the same as the earthly one. No one will be happy to vote for a political leader who will sleep in the parliament; while other leaders are strongly negotiating for better lives for their own followers. Political leaders never get support if they are not working hard; only the eloquent and powerful politicians win the hearts of many followers. The situation is the same as that of pastors. They have to represent their followers in a spiritual way and in the Heavenly parliament.

Once the followers are happy and satisfied, they automatically shower their spiritual religious leaders with gifts. They even support them in prayers. When everyone is sleeping, eagle religious leaders get out of their comfortable beds at night, and kneel down to pray for their congregation's well being. The Holy Spirit guides us through to pastors who are trustworthy, who can pray for our protection and salvation. The Holy spirits send us to religious leaders who will help us to be spiritually fulfilled. This explains why so many religious leaders are outstanding in preaching and teaching; however, people visit their churches once and never return. Being a good preacher is not enough. Preaching goes with strong faith and prayers. God created Pastors, priests, and religious leaders as spiritual candles. When their lights are brightly shining, people get attracted to their lights and so as our guardian Angels. When they pray less their lights become dim, and people move away from them slowly. Eagle church leaders do not wait for Sunday to pray, they pray most of the time. They don't have many friends for God is their greatest friend.

As I was conducting my own personal spiritual research, I learned that church leaders especially bishops, pastors, and priests are our

Heavenly representatives in a spiritual way. God sends them to pray and guide us at all times. If they don't, they might have to account to our Heavenly Father on the judgment day. As the servants of the Lord, they will have to account for why they did not support or pray for us during our times of need. Our Guardian Angels work closely with them. Once people are spiritually and emotionally uplifted, guardian Angels become happy.

Many people missed opportunities in their lives such as an important business deal, job interview, a test, or competitions. The time God sent their Angels to deliver the good news; those Angels were not spiritually strong. They couldn't fly and didn't arrive in time. When this particular person arrived at the competition or job interview, it was already late; because his Angel delivered the message late.

How many times people were promised great jobs, they even knew the interview questions in advance. However, they failed to express themselves during the interviews. They lost concentration and missed their last opportunities. It is because their guardian Angels were afraid to enter into the interview rooms with them, or their Angels were not even there. At times, people make mistake of not inviting God and He never sent His Angels to be there and guide them. Strong guardian Angels grab the opportunities for their own people. Guardian Angels work better when we support them in prayers. They are the Angels of our Heavenly Father and He sends them to watch over us while we are asleep and to keep us safe against the evil forces. There is a competition among the Angels. Every Angel wants to work hard and please God, but if we do not pray to support them they become weak. They leave us and move to people with peaceful minds. People with peaceful minds and spirits, burn and shine like candles in a spiritual way. Their brightness attracts the Angels.

There are people who are trying everything to improve their lives, but nothing happens. It is not because they are not wise, but it's because they have no spirit guards. The Holy Spirit is not active in their lives and they are not aware. These people find themselves not being liked by others for reasons unknown. Their lights are dim; people avoid and attack them for no reason. People would even go to a stage of hating them. Have you ever been in a situation where you met people for the first time and they rejected you? They might have said nothing but you felt it, and saw by their reactions. At times people think that they have bad luck, it isn't like that. They only need to pray, so they could become like spiritual bright candles that attract Angels.

Some people never invite God when they go to important business deals and job interviews. When people forget to invite Him, He never sends his Angels of wisdom, bravery, and courage to accompany them. He knows our needs but we have the responsibility to pray and invite Him. Many patients could not make it out of operation rooms, they died, not because doctors were incompetent, but because those patients or their families and relatives forgot to pray and invite God for their protection in time. They forgot to ask their Pastors to pray for them and the devil took advantage, instilled fear in them. Consequently, their lives ended up in the hospitals. At the end we blame God. Many times we blame God for our own mistakes and for the devil's tricks.

One night my Heavenly Father took me on a spiritual tour. I had a vision of an eagle. In that vision I saw myself transformed into a large eagle by the Lord. I was flying high up the mountains with my wings spreading widely. When I looked down I saw the largest mountains and hills. The earth was full of green trees and other plants. The vision felt like a real situation, and I truly felt like a real eagle. It was so harmonious flying up there and I could see so clearly and from a distance. The sky was so brightly clear and nothing seemed to obstruct me. My whole focus was on flying high over the highest mountains, hills, and deep oceans, and I never felt tired. I flew so lightly with those large wings, as if I wasn't in a form of a huge bird. I never felt any weight or experienced any difficulties when flying. I have never seen a creature in my whole life so huge like that. When I woke up, I prayed to thank God for the vision and ask for its revelation.

The clear eyes of an eagle were a reminder and a reflection of the vision of "an eye among the stars." It was a vision that I once had when I was seven years old. It also reminded me of the time when God chose me amongst other children to be an apple of his eye. That was the time I entered into a covenant with him, to serve the nations. To serve Him like Mary Magdalene who was one of the disciples. She was a woman who abandoned her own personal life for his name. He called me to be his eyes to the helpless and hopeless, and to wipe tears of those in pain, trouble, and frustration. He used a bright eye to symbolize my life as a bright candle, which would share its light with many. He transformed me into a tool that he used to watch over those in need. He watched over me at all times. He called me amongst other women in Zion Christian Church. He prepared me throughout my journey in Zion. When God saw that I was ready to be used. He then sent me to the African apostolic churches to spread the message of hope and salvation. He guided me throughout in establishing a ministry. God kept all his promises, and sent Pastors and Prophets within the church.

Eagles have a sharp sight; they clearly see things or situations from a distance. Through spiritual wisdom, I was alert most of the time and knew in advance if problems were coming my way, and I avoided them. I was most of the time spiritually alert, and could sense troubles and easily detect evil forces. I established a strong relationship with God by turning my focus from the tangible material things of this world. I gave less attention to things like; cars, houses, valuable furniture, and money. They were important, but I was less glued to them. I maintained the balance between my spiritual life and natural life. I knew that once I was too glued to material things, I would experience problems in my spiritual growth.

The devil uses valuable things to steal our attention from the spiritual world such as losing money, car accidents, and other valuable things. When we are deeply hurt, our spiritual eyes become blind and we are unable to see from a distance. The Holy Spirit doesn't settle on angry hearts. Our guardian angels are also very sensitive; they never come close to us when we are angry, they become afraid of us.

Feelings of sadness turn our third spiritual eye blind. Anger makes it impossible for us to sense the presence of the Holy Spirit. When I accepted God's calling, I tried hard to be humble most of the time. I avoided negative situations and negative people, so to maintain my spiritual connection and sight. When I was sad or deeply hurt, I never had visions. It was like my whole spiritual world was shut. The Holy Spirit works within peaceful minds and souls. God revealed many things to me: like people's problems, challenges and illnesses, even good thing about their lives and mine only on days when I was spiritually pure. As a servant of God I had to strive hard for spiritual purity, so He could reveal things about people's lives. It was my duty to deliver his message to his people. The spiritual eye forms the most important part of people's lives.

People have to pray hard to be able to see with their spiritual eyes. The spiritual eye enabled me to see in advance when my children would be sick and I prayed. I was able to feel and assess the level of people's sickness. I remember one boy phoned asking me to rush over to his home because his brother was sick. When I prayed for guidance and assessed his condition spiritually, I felt that he was only in a physical pain that could heal easily, and he wasn't going to die during that period. His condition needed medical attention only.

There was a price to pay when I started to see things with my spiritual eye. I lost meaning of the valuable things of life. I felt like a total stranger in this world. Situations that people felt that were important became meaningless to me. I felt so sad when people died but I could not attend funerals, not because I was lazy or didn't want to give my physical support, but because I only had to pray for the souls to rest in peace, as I was guided by the Holy Spirit. None of my friends, neighbors, and some church members could understand that type of behavior; I lived in isolation and in silent places most of the time. Physical, I could be part of funerals and other social gatherings, but spiritually I was with them. I cared a lot about people's spiritual wellbeing. When they were sick, I supported them spiritually because I knew that once they were spiritually fine they would automatically heal physically. Being able to see clearly in a spiritual way enabled me to know whether people were naturally sick or whether their sickness was caused by demonic attacks.

Most people's illnesses were caused by the presence of the evil spirits. My spiritual eye enabled me to differentiate if sick people needed medical attention or just needed prayers. When I met sick people and prayed or supported them, they got healed, not because I had certain powers. I only touched them and God healed them. He gave me the wisdom to sense the nature of their illness. If they needed medication my Father would reveal to me, and I accompanied or advised them to visit the clinics or hospitals. Those who were mentally and emotionally disturbed, I accommodated them temporarily in my home for days. I counseled them indirectly through daily communication and they fully recovered. There were some, who were seriously ill, and I accommodated and supported them for some days and they recovered also. I prayed to God for wisdom, support, and courage, and He was always there.

When I accepted the calling, my Father said to me that Jesus Christ would use me to save lives. It became my responsibility to pray hard, meditate, and limit my eating habits, so I could see with my spiritual eye. I had to work hard to be spiritually pure. So the Holy Spirit could be with me and guide me at all times. I had to avoid destructions and maintain silence, so I could hear my Heavenly Father's voice. We all have been granted the power to see things in a spiritual world. The only challenge is how we live our lives so to gain God's trust.

When God send Angels into our lives to guide us, we are unable to see them or feel their presence because of anger and other destructions. When God sends them to us, and they find us being angry, they return with great disappointment. When they find us burning with anger they fear us and return. Holy Spirits work better in people who live mostly in silence and have peace within themselves. The devil also has angels whom he works with, and they are extremely clever. I also learned from one preacher that when God send His Angels, the devil's angels listen carefully and record the date and time. Before Gods' Angels arrive, the devil's angels come earlier to frustrate us. When our Heavenly Father's humble Angels arrive to deliver our gifts and messages, they find us filled with rage and anger, and they return sad.

Once we totally surrender to God, He reveals to us in advance bad things that we might come across or the devil's evil plans. When those evil moments arrive we act with wisdom. Think of a situation whereby you were on your way to an important business deal or an interview, before you get there you received a call that your child or someone close to you was involved in an accident. How would you feel? Would you be able to negotiate for an important business deal or answer all questions during the interview? You wouldn't be. Your whole attention would get captured by the devil's destructions and you would miss your last chance. The devil uses people close to us and our valuable things to make us lose important deals of our lives. Some plans and situations of our lives happen in a spiritual way and we are unable to notice them because of a lack of spiritual eyes, wisdom, and knowledge.

Once God is satisfied with your spiritual level, you will notice it by many visions. He will reveal to you in advance places where you will go, and what you will experience. He will warn you if there is something wrong with your car, house, or if you are facing danger. When you totally surrender to God it does not mean that you will not experience challenges. There will be challenges; however, he will give you the wisdom to deal with them, and to avoid the Devil's tricks.

Before I came in the United States to study, God revealed to me that I would come across serious challenges at work when I apply for study leave, but he would be with me, and that I would succeed at the end no matter what. He revealed that some of the officials within my department would try to deny me of paid study leave, and they did. My principal Elizabeth tried her best by accompanying me to the regional department to plead for my paid leave. My institutional support coordinator also tried; they both were turned down hopelessly. When that moment arrived I remained calm. The situation was completely hopeless. The Human Resource Manager assured me that I would never ever be granted a paid study leave for two years; "it had never happened, and it will never happen", she confirmed. Furthermore, she even quoted teachers who went on the same scholarship program before, and were not granted paid study leaves. They resigned because of unpaid leaves. She even recommended and signed for my unpaid leave though it was not her responsibility to do so. Procedurally, she was supposed to forward my application to the superintendant general for the final decision. Fortunately, during the ups and downs of my application process, I kept my head above the water, and remained as cool as a cucumber. For I knew my Heavenly Father of mount Zion had revealed the challenges that I would go through in advance. He asked me not to be afraid, for He would be with me and I would succeed at the end. My kids and those I adopted would have more than enough to eat and drink while I am abroad.

God revealed to me in a vision, I saw my leave application unapproved by the same woman. In the same vision again, I saw that application being destroyed, and a new one being approved for study with full pay. Finally, my study leave was approved with full pay for two years by the Superintendant General of the Department of Education; after having considered the curriculum needs, my motivations for a paid leave, motivation from my school, and my remarkable contributions in different schools and communities as a passionate developing educator. Before I arrived in the United States, God used Prophet Abel to deliver his message that he had already prepared everything for me in America. I should not be troubled in any way. God revealed the type of town house I would live in, and the college environment. When I arrived in the United States everything was exactly how God had revealed to me.

God has given each and every one of us eagle wings to fly. He has granted us the power and strength to spread our wings and fly everywhere. We just have to ask Him to renew our strength and help us to fly. The problems we encounter on daily basis in our societies, families, work, church, personal and business problems have chained us to earth and we are unable to fly high. These problems have locked us into cages. They have turned us into eagles caged in a domestic setup. People have great business ideas, they are sitting with qualifications in their drawers, but they cannot move. It is time to acknowledge our eagle wings and fly high. People have great potential to change their lives and those of other's but they are overpowered with fear and they are unable to fly.

My Father saved my life by spreading his wings and caught me before I fell down. When I was about to lose hope, strength, and courage after all the hardships and humiliations I went through. After that, He renewed my strength, and I started flying high like an eagle. Eagles are meant to fly high above all other birds. He helped me to regain my power and strength. He broke all the spiritual, financial, mental, and emotional chains of bondage in my life. For years, I was like a caged eagle and I wasn't aware. I learned from the teachings in Zion that the greatest thing to do in life is to fight for spiritual growth. Spiritual wisdom and growth is the key to everything. This is the most important area of our lives that opens our link to the spiritual world of the unseen.

I started having visions only when the Lord started to trust me. I also could feel the spiritual growth and difference in my life. I wasn't hundred percent perfect but at least I was in a good mental and emotional state. I felt the presence of the Holy Spirit at all times. I was able to hear his voice and listen. God is always there watching over us but He is unable to speak to us because our ears are blocked by too much focus into the material things. Each and every believer has the responsibility to pray for spiritual connection and growth.

Spiritual connection doesn't happen overnight. However, there are those fortunate ones who get immediate connection into the world of the unseen: when they acknowledge the presence of the Holy Spirit, accept salvation, and believe in God. Some people may take long praying and serving the lord before they could feel the presence of the Holy Spirit. Once a believer becomes spiritually connected, his/her focus changes from the material world into a meaningful spiritual life. Everyone in this world is destined by God to be an eagle that is meant to fly high with a clear vision. After the vision of an eagle, my life changed. I acknowledged my spiritual gifts, and served the purpose of God. I started flying high like never before.

The Holy Spirit does not work much in people who talk too much and unnecessarily. Talking to people is good but there has to be a limit. The Holy Spirit does not operate in people who talk nonstop. I once had an old woman who was my helper. She was looking after my kids. She talked so much, and I had to come up with a plan to avoid her without hurting her feelings. I had to wake up early every morning, and prepare for work. When she knocked at my door, I greeted her nicely and drove to work. Her whole mind was over crowded with lot of people's stories and gossips.

She was more like a community radio. I started to realize that talking was not only a habit but a problem. When she came in the morning and found me in the shower, she stood outside the shower door and started talking until I finished. She didn't care if I responded or not, her aim was to talk and deliver the latest community news.

If Christians could turn their focus to God, talk to him like that even if he is not responding, this world would have been a much happier place to live in. God wants us to establish a strong relationship with him by talking with him all the time. When you need advice, just tell him. When you need money tell him and trust him. When you have to face challenging moments in your life, ask for wisdom and clarity before telling people. Sometimes, He uses our minds to communicate with us. He brings thoughts into our minds and most people ignore them, because they think it's their own thoughts. When the Holy Spirit takes control, it makes it easy for us to distinguish between our own thoughts and God's thoughts. The devil also uses our minds, but prayers block him not to read our minds.

God transformed me into a huge eagle so I could spread my wings and I fly high beyond reasonable doubt. He made me fly high in front of my enemies. His Blessings showered in my life almost at the same time. They showered like a heavy storm of rain after years of drought, pain, humiliation, and isolation. God lifted me up in front of the nations, particularly in a place where people witnessed my fall. He stirred the eagles nest in my marriage life; when I was comfortable and had forgotten all about him. My whole life was turned upside down. At the Ultimate end, He gave me the strength to fly high up above the mountains where no ordinary men could see.

CHAPTER 8

THE CALL OF GOD: FOUNDING ST. MARY'S

One night while I was sleeping in a peaceful, silent, and harmonious place at the Head Quarters of the Zion Christian Church, in Moria; I had a vision. I heard God's voice. He said: "My child" and I replied: "Yes Father, I'm listening". He said: "look down there" and I looked. He further said: "What do you see?" I replied: "I can see the apostolic church members dressed in blue and white, some in Green and some in other colors". He said: "they are my children too, and I love them the way I love all the other children in the whole world. However, people humiliate them, undermine, and call them names." He said: "My child, I am sending you to join them, and preach the message of hope and salvation among them." He further said to me: "my child never be afraid, Jesus Christ will use you to save lives." When I woke up I was amazed, for I thought God wouldn't send me to the apostolic churches. I also didn't know how and when He would send me there.

I tried to forget the vision and continued with my life in the Zion Christian Church, for I knew that it would never be possible. I tried to keep quiet and ignore the vision, but it lay on my spirit like a heavy guilty burden. I had sleepless nights, and at times I got angry with God, why he wanted me to join the Zion Apostolic Churches. Personally, I had nothing against them except that I wasn't in favor of churches with uniforms. They identified themselves with blue, white, yellow, green, and other colors. I had a problem with their choice of uniform design, not with the colors. God's decisions are never challenged. His decision was final, and I had no choice. I got so frustrated and ill, but at the end, I had I to obey His will. I liked the Zion Apostolic church type of music. Some of my relatives were members of these apostolic churches too, but I never wished to be part of them.

I accepted God's calling and started living a life with a purpose. I gave Him total control of my life, unconditionally. I allowed Him to manage every single aspect of my life. He managed my budget, daily plan, and diary. I completely surrendered to him. I never had friends because there was no time to visit them anymore. I surrendered my life totally to the Almighty; and lived on faith and His promises. Everything I did for Him, I did it as if it was my last day. I never cared about what people said. Every day they criticized, mocked, and hit me with heart breaking words. I personally turned their negative words into spiritual stones of courage, and collected them all to build a house of safety and faith. So I would be safe during the period of storms. All their criticisms and judgments made me grow personally and spiritually strong day by day. What people didn't know by then was that I was fully aware of all the negative things they said about me. I kept quiet and prayed hard, asking my heavenly father to give me strength and deliver out of that situation. The negative treatment I received gave me all the reasons to pray every day and strengthen my relationship with my father.

When my marriage broke up, some people laughed and rejoiced, only a few sympathized with me. I joined the Zion Christian Church; they also gossiped. I had a baby girl, Keamogetse, people kept on talking. I helped poor children and they said I was overdoing community work and continued to gossip. I created jobs and established business for youth, they gossiped, saying that I was wasting my time. I was involved in the school development activities and management issues; they called me a lazy office teacher. God granted me the wisdom and the strength to be involved in many activities. He blessed everything that I laid my hands on, with the illustrious difference that captured the attention of the education department and the American embassy. I thought of Noah when God asked him to build the ark. People criticized him, but he continued with his work, for He knew that he would be safe during the time of storm. I moved from Zion Christian Church and established the ministry of St Mary's Inter Denominational, and people never stopped talking. They called me names and said I was living a confused life. Some of my formed Zion priests and members, who knew me, said I was going crazy. They said I wasn't even a type of a ministry material young woman. Nothing they said made me lose focus; I served my Heavenly Father with all my heart, despite all the challenges and everything.

Through God's power I managed to heal the sick and changed lives. I used all the criticisms, gossips, and humiliation as word of encouragement to build a house for my Lord. I worked so hard for my father. I made a remarkable difference in people's lives. I didn't even care or count. Perhaps God let it happen for a purpose, so I could wait for the right time. On my eleventh year of teaching and serving the Lord, blessings showered like a rain. He lifted me up in front of everyone. When the American Embassy recognized my efforts and granted me a scholarship to study in America. They then started to realize that all I did was for the best. God delivered his promises and rewarded me at the end.

My journey of life as a young woman made me learn the importance of total surrendering unto the Lord. I turned a deaf ear to all the criticisms, gossips, and humiliations I went through. His purpose became my first priority. I gave myself unto Him as his servant. My daily job became His. Before I went to work I knelt down to invite him to accompany me, and to give me the courage to face the challenges of each and every day. During the hard times I prayed, and waited patiently for him to answer. When I prayed and asked for money or something, I never rushed to the bank or to people to borrow money, I waited patiently for his guidance. I gave him a chance to respond for I understood that He was quick to hear and took time to answer.

Life taught me that it doesn't matter how long it takes to suffer and go through difficulties and challenges, for at the end God answers and delivers his promises. I never allowed my financial problems to stand in my way. My financial life deteriorated, it became worse. I lived a life that had meaning to God but meaningless to the people of this material world. To them I was more like an alien or a total stranger. Everything I did for the love of God, they regarded it as madness. They regarded my work as foolish, but deep down I knew I had a covenant with God. When I was at the Zion Christian Church, He asked me to help those in need, even if it meant giving my last piece of bread to them. He promised me that he would provide for my needs and one day I would forget all the difficulties and rejoice. I don't think I was the only one whom God asked to help the needy and pray for the sick and helpless on earth, or at the Zion Christian Church. I still believe He asked millions; however, people decided to ignore His word and live their own lives for reasons known to them.

When God challenged me to move from the Zion Christian Church to St.' Mary's Inter Denomination Ministry, I prayed hard trying to convince him to choose any of his better children among the millions within the Zion church, and send them to the apostolic. By better children of God I meant those who bragged most of the time within the church, saying that they were the only best children of God. When I compared their lives with my own, I noticed that God loved them so much. He never asked them to help the helpless and those in need and in pain. They lived and enjoyed their lives to the fullest, and never cared less about helping others.

There were times when I felt that My Heavenly Father was unkind to me. I felt that He never cared if I was tired or had no money. At times he woke me up in the middle of the night or any time to pray. I did as the Holy Spirit guided me, for I never wanted to disappoint my Heavenly Father. He sent me to many places, and never cared how much I had in my pocket. I depended on borrowing money from my colleagues and other women organizations and they charged interests, so I could travel to places where He wanted me to go. Some month ends meant nothing to me. When people had their salaries, I had no money. At the end of the month, when my colleagues and other workers bought groceries for their families, clothes, and went out to restaurants, I couldn't. I had to repay those debts I owed with interests. At times I told people that they were fortunate because they could make plans about their lives and adhere to them. They drew their own budgets and spent accordingly, and that was not possible in my life. I never bothered to draw up my own daily plan or budget. I couldn't manage my own diary either. God had total control over my life, it was not easy; I accepted and made peace with that.

I travelled to Pietersburg almost every month to pray, and it was very far from where I lived. I never wanted to question or challenge God in any way. I only followed his commandments and lived under his guidance. One man from the Zion church once told me not to do everything that the Lord asked me to do, he advised me to tell God that I am tired or I don't have money. The man tried to advise me not to help children from the community, and those living in the streets. He said that I was wasting my money. I should save money for my own children. It was a dream for me to live my own way, enjoy my salary, but my Heavenly Father's purpose was my priority. My own life suffered, and I was in serious debts, but never gave up. My children never had decent life like other children. However, I knew one day they will live a better life. I knew God had put me through that situation to prepare me for better tasks in the future. I had faith that one day I would be happy and free. I perfectly understood, and knew that my tears wouldn't last for long. I had faith that God will give me joy that will last forever. My children will become the happiest one day.

One morning when I woke up my life was completely different. I became a totally different person; my journey to Zion came to a sudden end. People might not believe me or understand how I felt, but it was painful. My whole life became filled with pain, frustration, and confusion. I felt so totally different; I felt like a stranger in my own Father's land. When darkness fell or the night approached, I got terrified. I felt like running away to a brightly lit place where I could hide from the terrors of the night. I may not tell exactly why my Lord let all that happen to me, but I knew he had a reason. I was troubled by terrifying visions. I saw creatures that I couldn't describe. I screamed in the middle of the night, jumped out of my bed, and sat down flat on the floor just to guard my own life and pray.

Even though I was terrified deep down, I knew I was like Jonah from the bible when he ignored God's purpose. He was a disobedient prophet who took his own way when God sent him, and was swallowed by the whale. God had allowed all these terrifying things to happen to me because it was time for me to move from the Zion Christian Church to Apostolic church, but I refused. I was afraid of facing humiliations and criticisms in his name. I knew my own brothers and sisters from Zion and my community would never stop criticizing me that I move to a low class church of the apostolic. However, I knew that in my Father's house there is no low class, no race, and no color.

At night I was overwhelmed with endless visions. When other people woke up, I felt so exhausted, with terrible headache. Most of those visions were educational in a spiritual way, but they were too many. I couldn't cope and I couldn't go to work for almost three months. These visions were more like a spiritual learning journey. I learned about different challenges and problems faced by people on earth; their different illnesses and cure, curses and how to break them. Personally I felt like God was punishing me because I didn't want to establish a ministry within the apostolic communities. Visions that frustrated me the most were the ones when he revealed to me the different traditional healing practices. That was the last thing I wanted to do, or know about. He revealed to me many different healing processes including how to pray for and heal the people. He let all that happen to me because of my stubbornness to serve his purpose. I was ashamed and afraid that people will criticize me. I asked myself questions like "who would see me being a prophet or a spiritual healer, especially at my age and as a young teacher. I never wanted any of those gifts. I cried in some nights, praying God to take away those gifts, and give them to desperate people out there who needed them, and he never listened.

I registered for a degree in Psychology because I thought God would let me serve his purpose through the Psychological counseling practice. I was hoping to use those gifts in a psychological practice, as it would have looked more professional and stylish, but all my attempts to run away from God's calling were vain. I registered twice but never succeeded. After failing in Psychology, I tried community work, hoping He would be pleased and take away his spiritual gifts. He was never pleased and never listened. Nothing I did seemed to please God.

Community work had always been my favorite since I was part of the Zion church. I worked harder than before, but my Father was never happy, and in fact one would say he was not even interested. I never wanted to be a church founder, or a leader, or anything that had to do with the church; for I knew how people were fighting for positions and power within the churches. I drained all my energy into community work, hoping God would change his mind about his purpose about my life, but he never did. In the afternoons when all teachers were going to their homes to cook for their families and enjoy the rest of the afternoons, I travelled to different communities, and shared my business and counseling skills with unemployed youth.

I did everything as if it was my last day. I recruited other educators to those communities, and they supported me. The organizations got established, and youth started their businesses. Children from disadvantaged families and those living in the streets were offered food on certain days. The sad thing was that the meals received by some of those children served as the only meal they had for the day. I invited some of the children to my home that were sick; some I washed their wounds and took them to health centers. I counseled and prayed for them, helped some of them at their schools, homes, and they all got healed and adapted to normal life through God's power. I shared everything I had with them and those I adopted from the community. At times we went to bed with no electricity; however, the love of God shone through my house.

My whole time and money were consumed by my commitment in the community. I registered for short courses on community economic development, trauma debriefing, and victim empowerment; so I could empower youth. My own family life suffered but I never felt troubled, it was all peaceful. I couldn't have a decent meal with my children. I depended on borrowing money from my colleagues with the interests; however, life went on and on, and I felt so spiritually fulfilled.

Helping children and making a noticeable difference in the community made me feel like I had shared something great and special. I never cared about what the people said for I knew people were never happy or satisfied, and they never stop talking and gossiping. Whether one does good or bad, talks and gossips continue. I taught my own kids to love and accept other children who came to visit, or temporarily stay with us for some reasons. Sometimes my house was so overcrowded and I could see my neighbors were not happy as I lived in town cluster homes.

These children didn't care about the luxuries of beautiful beds; sleeping on the floor or on mats with few blankets was more than enough. They needed nothing but love; they didn't make my house dirty or eat all my delicious meals in the fridge. All they needed was to be loved. I always knew that once they were emotionally and physically healed, they would peacefully return to their homes. I knew my Father brought them for a purpose. My house might not have been as materially well equipped and beautiful as those of my colleagues, friend and neighbors, but I knew in my heart that there was love and warmth inside. I had no doubt that my Heavenly Father of mount Zion was watching over me, and one day it will become one of the most beautiful houses ever.

Every day I had a challenge to face. One afternoon, when I arrived home from work, I received a call. A Priest from Zimbabwe whom I had known for a long time called me. He was in prison and he asked me to bail him out. He said he was wrongly arrested for a crime he had not committed. I never allowed him to finish his story over the phone, and I told him I didn't have money. He told me the name of the prison where he was arrested, and I dropped the phone. By that time I was in serious debts. My whole life was a mess financially. My salary couldn't cover all the debts. I spoke out loudly saying: "Father it's too much now, I am not Jesus Christ to save all these people." I couldn't take it anymore, due to the fact that the previous month I helped one family with money for the burial. The same month one student was about to be deregistered at the University, he needed registration fees, and I helped him out. When Mr. Sabin, in Prison spoke with me, he indicated that he could only recall my number from all the numbers of people he knew. He didn't have a cell phone by then, he called from a public phone. That was strange to me because we never talked for the past five years. I didn't even have his cell phone numbers.

Choosing to be an instrument of God was not an easy task. He made me go through tests and challenging situations of life for a purpose. Immediately after I had dropped the phone after talking with Mr. Sabin, I felt extremely tired and laid on my bed for a nap. I had a vision, God asked me to help Sabin out of prison. He revealed to me to go to Freda, one of my friends, and ask her to lend me money so I could go to Sun City prison. When I woke up, I was not happy. Actually I cried a lot because I was now tired from borrowing money from people. I was tired of gossips and financial constraints. Despite all the challenges, I became more like an obedient child and did what the Lord asked me to do.

Freda agreed to lend me some money for the bail, and she accompanied me to the Sun City prison together with my uncle, aunt, and cousin. It was very far from where I lived, and I had never heard or seen it before. I did not even know where it was located. I asked for directions and invited God to be with us throughout the journey, finally we arrived safely. When we got there the Prison warders told us that they would not let us in, as it wasn't a day for visitors. I tried to beg them and convince them that we were from very far and that we only needed to pay Mr. Sabin's bail.

They agreed to accept the bail but when they checked into their computer records, they realized that the money I brought wasn't enough. It was only half of the bail. They informed us that we were not allowed to see the man. Furthermore, they would not be able to help us since our money was not enough. I left the office with disappointment and shame. I spoke with God silently in my heart and said: "Father, how could you let me down like this, you had sent me to this prison for nothing." I was also afraid that Freda will mock me that I lied about God, or my visions were not real because when I asked her to lend me money, I told her that I had a vision, God sent me to her to borrow money to bail out Mr. Sabin."

Ultimately, I gave up and we went to the parking to drive back home. Miracles happen when we least expected them. When I was about to start my car and drove back home, I received a call from my uncle who was a prison warder in another Prison. I may not know what pressured him to think of calling me at that particular time of need and desperation, but I believed he was driven by the power of God. I answered the phone and explained the situation. Immediately he gave me the telephone numbers of the Director of Sun City Prison. I called him, and to my surprise he told me that he had been waiting for us for the whole day to pay half of the bail. I was surprised when he mentioned that Mr. Sabin's younger brother was within the prison office. He came in the morning with half of the bail and had been waiting there for the whole day.

I was very amazed at how God had performed His miracle. I was surprised because Mr. Sabin didn't know that we were coming on that day. The last time we spoke over the phone, I told him that I would not be able to help him out with bail. Finally, Mr. Sabin was freed. I may not tell if He was wrongly arrested or not, for it wasn't my place to judge. Moreover, my Father didn't send me to Prison to interrogate Mr. Sabin. My purpose for the day was to set him free only for reasons known to God. He was not the only person I helped out of Prison; there were others in different prisons. I did that out of love and was only serving the purpose of My Heavenly Father.

One day when I was within the Zion church crying silently about the challenges I was going through, the Lord sent a prophet to reveal to me that the current storms in my life will be over soon, and I will find joy and peace. I cannot recall how many children and youth lived in my house for all those years; however, I was grateful that when they left my home, they were completely healed in many ways and accordingly. Some could even stand up on their own feet independently, seek employment, and return to their families. Did all my efforts make God change his plan about establishing a ministry? No, he didn't. He kept on requesting me to establish a ministry.

The more I refused to establish a ministry, the more I felt like I had stroke attacks at night. I was so terrified that I never thought I would recover when I woke up in the morning. Some nights, I sat on the floor being scared to sleep. At times, I felt like my whole body was filled with terrible cramps that I couldn't move my body. At times I wanted to scream out of fear, but my voice was gone. I felt like I wasn't going to recover in the morning. Some nights I woke up screaming half of my body feeling partly not functioning. I couldn't move any part of my body, and had no voice to shout for help; however, my mind was working. I tried to pray but those attacks lasted for almost the whole night. I couldn't stop tears from my eyes.

I consulted with Psychiatrists and Psychologists for help, and they prescribed some strong medication that enabled me to sleep, but I couldn't go to work. The medication made me more tired when I woke up. At times when I met people God revealed to me the nature of their illnesses and remedies, but I kept quiet because I was ashamed. When I kept quiet and not telling them I got affected by their illnesses. That was one of the things that made me feel like I was being punished for not accepting God's calling. When I met people who suffered from headaches or stomach illness, and I didn't tell them what the Lord revealed to me, I felt their illnesses. It became worse that I couldn't even drive. In some places I could sense the demonic spirits, and I had to park my car and pray silently. If not, I would not be able to move my body or drive. When people saw my car parked, they would think I was having a rest, not knowing that I was trying to handle the spiritual pressure.

At the end I got confined to my home, as going out would mean problems. I cried all the time, not because I was hurt but the spiritual pressure was too much. When I felt the pressure, tears just swelled like water from my eyes. I remember one day I tried to force myself to work, and when I was in the office, I felt spiritually pressured. I tried to be strong and hide it, but the tears were so uncontrollable. One of my colleagues, Rita, tried to comfort me because she thought I had problems or I was hurt, but I wasn't. Despite all the difficulties I kept on refusing to let myself be used by God.

When I visited the Psychiatrist for more sleeping medication, he advised and suggested that I accept God's calling and serve his purpose, but I never changed my mind. He gave me an example, that some of the people who were insane in mental hospitals had almost the same calling as mine, but they refused and got worse. For once, I agreed with him because I could partly feel that my mind was affected by medication. I started to suffer from occasional memory loss and lack concentration. Every day I got extremely exhausted, I slept all day and night and not going to work.

I met a woman who was a spiritual healer, and she looked at me as if she was shocked. She asked for my name and about the ethnic group that I came from. I told her my name and she repeated the same questions again. She only shook her head and said: "My child, you are truly gifted. Some years to come, you will travel to different countries and provinces to pray for the nations, and spread the message of salvation". I got more frustrated because I never wanted even a single gift. She even told me that I'm trying to run away but I won't runaway forever.

One morning when I woke up, I felt spiritually free to visit my church of the Zion Christian after three months of staying alone at home feeling sick. I was feeling better by then, and thought it was time that I approached my priests and tell them about my problem. I went to them hoping that they would ask God to take away those spiritual gifts that He imposed on me and give them to those who deserved them. They listened and advised me to seek God's revelation. My Father never changed his mind; He repeated the same thing all the time. I doubted the Prophetic revelation. I went to another Zion church which was far from my area to seek prophetic revelation again, and I was told the same thing.

Finally, I got strength and drove miles to Pietersburg at Moria, which was my last hope. When I got there, I cried for the whole day to the priests asking them to help me, but instead they mocked me. They told me that I was telling lies, and I was trying to make an excuse of leaving the church. They told me that it had never happened in the history of the church, and it will never be possible that God could guide a woman to establish a ministry, and pray for the sick. I cried a lot and asked them to pray for me, and request God to take away those spiritual gifts, or that confusion, but they never listened.

Nothing they said made me leave the church arrogantly, I waited patiently for I knew that God has his own ways and He would make a way for me. Before I left my home to Pietersburg, God revealed to me that the High Priest who was the leader of Brass band would help me there. When I arrived the five priests who were in charge by then took me from pillar to post, but my hope was never lost. Fortunately, as I was sitting at the office bench crying helplessly, the Brass band leader showed up. I related my story crying and he referred me back to those Priests in a humble way, as they were the ones assigned to make major church decisions for that particular day. When I returned to ask them to pray for me, they broke my heart. If I had to measure the tears I shed from my eyes on that day, many buckets would be filled. They kept on telling me that I was making excuses to leave the church, and I was telling lies about God. Besides, they said that it was impossible for a woman to have the gifts of praying and healing.

At the end of the day they came to an agreement and recorded that I could move from Zion to the Apostolic. At least God reached their hearts and minds. They recorded in the books of the church on

26 April 2008 that I could take my eagle blood and fly back home to the Apostolic Church and serve the purpose of God. One of them said there was nothing they could do to change the plan of God about my life. I returned to the leader of the brass band and told him that I would be going home to establish a ministry. He gave his blessings and told me to return if I needed help.

On Sunday morning when I was listening to the church brass band, I looked up at the mountains where the king of Zion lived and I saw an amazing view. I saw a beautiful sight ever that made me feel so encouraged, and free to go and join the apostolic family. I saw two flags hung up, one was blue in color and one was white. I felt it was God's sign to bid me farewell to the apostolic churches to serve his purpose. Those were the two flags colors I never expected at his place, and it was for the first time in my life at Zion that I witnessed that. I was with my spiritual brother, Steven, and he witnessed those flags and he was also truly humbled and amazed by that sight. We both believed it was God's way to clear my paths. The type of blue and white on the flags were the most dominant colors used by the Apostolic. It was not the type of blue used in Zion female choir uniform.

Not every man or every woman would face the high priests of the Zion Christian church and inform them that they are moving out of the church. I believe that I was driven by the power of faith and the Holy Spirit to have the courage to face the priests. On my way from Pietersburg, I went to my local priests in Lichtenburg to inform them that finally I have accepted the calling, and have been released. One of the Priests (late) who was the head of the church by then, said to me: "My child, may God bless you for you are the first child in my whole life since I was a priest in Zion to come and inform us that you are moving out from Zion to Apostolic." I made peace and returned home to my late grandmother's place, Oudora, where I grew up, a place in which I saw an eye among the stars. I established the ministry in her yard. My cousin, Hidy, moved out from Zion also and joined me at the new ministry. My younger Sister, Florence, also joined and later all my extended family members and some of my relatives followed.

The majority of the children and people I used to help before also joined me voluntarily for reasons known to them and God. I believe God's prophesy was fulfilled as He promised me that once I establish the church, he will sent people who will help me to pray. I also remember that one of the reasons I was hesitant to receive God's calling was that I told him that I didn't know how to preach and pray. He promised that he will guide me, send the congregation, prophets, and pastors. He further promised that He will send Highest Priests, Bishops, and honorable dignitaries from around the world who will voluntarily help with registration of the Church.

Before I went to St. Mary's Inter Denominational Apostolic Ministry, I had a covenant with my Heavenly Father. We agreed upon the following: the church uniform would be totally different from those of other Apostolic Churches. Our weekly prayer meeting days would be different from that of other churches; we will meet on Tuesdays and Sundays. These promises were followed by the questions I asked my Father. I also told Him that I wasn't comfortable with the old Apostolic Church uniform design. He revealed a different uniform design which I was comfortable with, and which other members also liked. My father explained that St Mary's is a spiritual hospital, members were the nurses, and their uniform was designed in a dignified way. He revealed a cape (poncho) that I wore and it distinguished me from other members for reasons known to him. My cape was different from the Priests gowns; I had to put it around with the church uniform, and it was also smartly designed. When it was revealed to me my father said I am the matron of the hospital, St Mary's. He never said I am the owner of the church, as the church belongs to Him. A matron of the Hospital's duty is to oversee and guide the nurses. She needs to consult with the Owner of the Hospital at all times, giving progress reports, and seeking wisdom and advise. What amazed me the most was that other apostolic members and churches were not comfortable to mix with our church members; however, they showed lot of admiration and respect. Some people kept on asking what kind of a church St Mary's was. Some asked if we were the Roman Catholic, the Zion Christian, and Apostolic or Born agains. No one could understand what kind of church St Mary was; it was flexible and integrated many practices to accommodate everyone. The secret behind the foundation of St Mary's was with the owner, My Heavenly Father.

All the people who followed me at St. Mary's came voluntarily for reasons known to them and God. God sent me priests and prophets, and that made some of my former local Zion members unhappy. They accused me that St. Mary's imitated Zion for reasons known by them. I remained silent for I understood that those weren't my battles to fight. When I established the ministry, my uncle and aunt, Mr. and Mrs. Mochawe, moved from their church. They joined at St.' Mary's. Mr Mochawe was a High priest from his former church. God revealed to me to approach one priest, Mr. R. Kerileng, to request some guidance from him on some of the apostolic church practices. He was from the St.' Paul's Apostolic Church and had experience; he visited occasionally and worked with Rev M. Mochawe. Some priest came voluntarily, and I believe they were sent by God.

I met with the first church Prophet Abel Kgale, when he was very sick. He was a member of the Zion Christian Church by then. One

Priest of Zion church called one evening asking me to take Abel to the Hospital. He said that there was nothing that he could do to help Abel; his condition was serious. I tested my God of impossibilities and he answered my prayers instantly and beyond reasonable doubt. I prayed for Abel and he got healed completely, and he followed me at St.' Mary's. I tested my God several times in situations that everyone including myself; though it was impossible. However, He performed his miracles. Many children and people got healed completely when I prayed with them, not because I had powers but when I touched them, God used me and healed them.

I was once accused by some of my former local Priests of Zion that I had stolen healing water from their church to heal people. I cared less because I knew that God had anointed me since I was a little girl. When I was only ten years old my grandmother used to call me whenever she was sick, and asked me to give her some water. She felt better, and that's why she said that I should become a nurse when I complete my high school.

At St. Mary's I became a simple member, not a pastor. My Heavenly Father and I had a covenant to establish the church for him not for myself. It wasn't my church; it was His. My duty was to pray for and heal people through his will. I only gave people answers about their lives. Despite, he sent Priests and Prophets and they were doing well. My duty was to advise them when there was a need only. I was guided by the Holy Spirit at all times, and they listened to me even though I was still young. I was on my early thirties. That kind of arrangement didn't sound good to other neighboring church leaders. They could not understand why I was the founder, and I was not a Priest or a pastor. They believed and knew that most people who founded churches automatically became bishops, or pastors of those very churches, and that was different in my case. I knew that I would become a pastor, or take any position within the church at the right time chosen by the lord. If there was a way that I could have given someone the title of being the founder of the church, I would have given it a long time ago. Unfortunately, it was not possible. Some things were created by God for a purpose, and can never be changed in anyway. I know I am being forward to compare myself with Jesus, but I know He wouldn't mind. Jesus Christ embarked on a public ministry, and it is not mentioned in the bible if he became a high priest or a pastor of the ministry. It is only written that people witnessed his miracles and followed Him. He was sent by God and was guided by the Holy Spirit.

When I left for America, the church continued as usual, people got healed even in my absence. The Holy Spirit guided them throughout when I was away. I was miles and miles away from them physically; however, we were all strongly connected in a spiritual way, and like never before.

Finally, I accepted God's calling, made peace with my inner self to be an instrument of God. I acknowledged and appreciated my spiritual gifts. I named the church after Mary the mother of Jesus, to spiritually acknowledge the presence of a woman who was chosen among all the women to give birth to our personal savior, Jesus Christ. The name Mary also includes Mary Magdalene, a woman disciple who sacrificed her own personal life and followed Jesus Christ. Even though my former local Zion brothers and sisters, whom I loved so much judged me, saying a woman cannot establish a ministry and can never pray for the sick, however, my Heavenly Father and the members of St.' Mary's never judged me in any way. Nothing and no one in this world will ever make me forget what the Lord of Mount Zion has done for me. Zion will forever be my home of courage and wisdom. I will keep on knocking at the greatest gate and the doors of Zion until they are opened.

VISITING THE AUTHOR

Mosebodi Betty Metswamere dedicated her spare time travelling to different communities helping vulnerable youth and children. She offered emotional and psychological support to the children and other victims of crime and violence. In her whole teaching career, she never had time to rest and never lived for herself. During that period, God promised her that one day she would be rewarded and would get to rest like all other teachers. Indeed, God delivered his promises.

Due to her passion and dedication to change the lives of others in different communities, she sacrificed her time and studied both Public Health and Community Psychology, and Victim Empowerment and Support (VEP) at the University of South Africa. Among other things, she established Non Profit Organizations (Agisanang & Regololosegile) which were vital in social crime prevention, poverty alleviation, and economic empowerment for both youth and children. Children from disadvantaged families and those living in the streets were offered meals and recreational activities. Youth were empowered to run their businesses. Some were trained to serve in the corporate and government sectors. Her interest in serving the community was also spurred by the underprivileged economic conditions of the children she taught, and the high rate of unemployment of youth within the Ngaka Modiri Molema District particularly in Lichtenburg. In addition, she volunteered in the South African Depression and Anxiety Group (SADAG) as a support group leader.

Ms. Metswamere spent most of her childhood alone and in isolation communicating with her imaginary friend "God". During her childhood, God revealed her future and career path through dreams and visions, but never revealed her spiritual purpose. Sibu enjoyed her strong relationship with God, but she never thought that God had a great mission about her life. She was not aware that she had spiritual gifts in healing, encouraging, and changing the lives of many people. She loved God, but never wanted any spiritual gifts, or any purpose which involved praying for the sick and prophetic Ministry.

After completing her studies, Sibu was employed as a school teacher, and got married. She then started living a selfish life, and failed to remember her childhood imaginary friend "God". Sibu's husband became her source of strength and support. She completely forgot about her imaginary friend. There was total communication breakdown between Sibu and her imaginary friend. After some time, God sent a messenger to deliver the prophetic message to Sibu that her luxurious life will come to an end. Within a month, the prophecy was fulfilled. Her marriage broke apart, and her whole life lost its meaning. She started facing serious financial, spiritual, personal, and emotional challenges.

At the ultimate end, Ms. Metswamere surrendered completely unto the Lord and established St. Mary's Inter Denominational Ministry at Bodibe Village (Rakgolo Section). She moved from the Zion Christian Church and joined the minority African apostolic churches to spread the message of Hope and salvation.

mosebodi1@gmail.com